Wicked
Girl

Wicked Girl

JEANIE DOYLE

MIRROR BOOKS

First published by Mirror Books in 2020

Mirror Books is part of Reach plc
10 Lower Thames Street
London EC3R 6EN

www.mirrorbooks.co.uk

ISBN 978-1-912624-25-6

Typeset by Danny Lyle

Printed and bound in Great Britain by
CPI Group (UK) Ltd, Croydon, CR0 4YY

A CIP catalogue record for this book is available from the British Library.

Every effort has been made to fulfil requirements with regard to
reproducing copyright material. The author and publisher will be
glad to rectify any omissions at the earliest opportunity.

1 3 5 7 9 10 8 6 4 2

Cover image: © Getty Images

This book is dedicated to all the children that passed through my home and my family's life – thank you for trusting us and teaching us resilience!

Also to my wonderful husband and children – thank you for your unfailing patience, love and nurturing of those we chose to live with you.

Introduction

My name is Jeanie Doyle, and I have been a foster parent
– mother and grandmother – for 20 years.

I have cared for well over 100 children and young
adults, and I remember each one and their stories vividly.

Some I cared for very briefly, just overnight, others for
several years, and my affection for and connection with
many of them has continued well into their adult lives.

The cases I reveal here are all based on true experiences,
but I have changed names and some details to protect the
identities of the children I looked after as they try to build
new lives with jobs, homes and families of their own.

When I look back on those turbulent years, I often
wonder how my husband, our three children and I got
through it. The thing is, it's not a separate job, something
I did that was apart from my family. They had to be
involved as well, to accept it as part of their lives, otherwise
it wouldn't have worked.

Fostering is something that my husband Bill and I did as a couple, and definitely as a family. You have to rely on each other at different times.

My hope is that other people will see the challenges that yes, you do need to be aware of, but also the joys that offering a home to children when they need it most can bring into your own life.

Looking back, it was a wonderful thing to do. There were times when I struggled, when it almost tipped me over the edge into giving up. At moments like that I thought I'd made a mistake. But I never gave up on anyone, no matter how tough and trying they or their situation were.

In the long run I believe that if it was for one year, one month, one week, or even one night, if we kept one child safe and gave them a glimmer of hope, it was always worth it.

As an inspirational therapist I know tells me, every moment with that child would have been a moment of safety and security.

"They would have gleaned from that what they needed to go forward in life," she said. "You gave them that, Jeanie. You nurtured them and restored their trust. You helped them to believe in themselves and to thrive."

I take great comfort in her words. For me, this is what it continues to be all about: breaking a pattern of abuse, showing kindness and affection to children who have been neglected and brutalised, offering them a calm, stable routine. It's about giving them not only hope, but also the emotional strength to grow into happy, healthy adults.

Introduction

I thank them for giving me that chance. And I dedicate this book to them, my husband Bill and our children for playing their part in helping to mend those damaged young lives.

Prologue

A small huddled figure in a red anorak creeps down a quiet side street, throwing furtive glances over her shoulder. She is clutching a round wicker basket close to her chest. As she quickens her pace, her breath forms a white mist in the frozen air and tendrils of her long black hair escape from her quilted hood.

She darts though the deserted alleyways, oblivious to the twinkling Christmas lights shining cheerfully through the frosted window panes of cosy, warm homes.

She can feel her heart pounding now, beating a rhythm with the heavy chimes of the church clock as it strikes midnight. Its ominous toll seems to echo like a judgment and her pale cheeks flush with shame. May God forgive her for what she is about to do.

Suddenly a black shape darts across her path, hissing like a snake, two amber eyes fixing her with an accusing stare. She only breathes again when the silky black cat melts into the night.

At the foot of the stone church steps, she stops and looks around. There is nothing moving in the deserted streets around her. She strains to listen: just the murmur of a breeze and the distant strains of a drunken reveller tipped out of a pub somewhere in the inky beyond.

She climbs the steps, gently places the basket in the porch and reaches in to smooth the blanket lying on top. Her hands, swollen from the cold, look red raw against the lacy white wool. She nudges the basket carefully into the far corner of the porch, where strands of ivy have begun to snake their way up the arched wooden door.

She turns away and starts to run. Then, just as abruptly, she stops and stares back at the abandoned bundle, so vulnerable and lonely on the cold, hard stone.

Taking off her anorak, she cloaks it tenderly around the basket. "You'll be alright," she whispers.

With her arms now released from the weight she has carried hurriedly through the night, she races away.

Only now do the tears fall. Despairing sobs shudder through her frail body, echo around the streets and then fade into the darkness.

Our Festive Baby

We all agreed that this year's tree was a triumph. It was big, it was bright, it was groaning with baubles and tinsel – just as it should be. After last year's arty departure into a strictly white and gold tree, we were back to the usual "throw it all on" multi-coloured extravagance that we had come to love and expect from our local church hall in Salford.

The fairy lights were twinkling merrily as Boney M's festive hit *Mary's Boy Child* rang out over the crackling loudspeaker. It was 1978, a year that would prove a dramatic turning point for me and my family, and it all began with a baby born to a young teenage mum.

On that crisp winter's night just before everything changed, my husband Bill and I watched Stevie, the youngest of our three children, play the part of a shepherd in his school Nativity play. We were bursting with pride when he shyly took his bow, alongside his classmates, to passionate applause from all the beaming parents in the audience.

"Mum! Dad!" Stevie cried, charging through the crowd towards us in the costume I'd made from an old sheet and a checked tea-towel.

"Well done, love," I said, ruffling his corkscrew curls and planting a sloppy kiss on his caramel-smooth cheek. "You were brilliant."

"Mam!" he grinned self-consciously, his brown eyes sparkling as he rubbed the smudge of pink lipstick off his face.

He was only eight years old, yet I noticed that he was already becoming embarrassed by displays of affection in front of his school pals, dressed that night as crook-wielding shepherds, kings in false beards, woolly white lambs, and the tallest – and cheekiest – boy in the school playing a very chatty Angel Gabriel in a silver tinsel halo.

Despite his protests at my earlier attempt to kiss him, Stevie wasn't too old to hitch a ride on his dad's shoulders.

"Come here, buster," laughed Bill, scooping him up and hoisting him on to his back. "Let's go find your sisters."

As I watched my 6ft 4in gentle giant of a husband amble off with our chestnut-haired son to scour the room for his sisters Sophie and Sarah, I wanted to pause that moment forever.

I knew how lucky I was. Being a mum and having a family was just what I'd always wanted. Something, at one point, I thought I might never have.

I watched as the kids swarmed towards the tree, where piles of presents in shiny paper were waiting for them under the branches.

"Form an orderly queue," ordered Santa, sounding suspiciously like the officious young Mr Thomson, one of Stevie's teachers.

"Ho ho ho!" he boomed as the giggling youngsters, seeing straight through his disguise, tore open their parcels.

When I looked at Bill and our three happy, healthy kids, I knew I couldn't have asked for a better Christmas gift. But what made me feel even happier was knowing that in the new year, we would be welcoming another youngster into our home – our first foster child.

Bill and I had gone through the statutory training and suitability checks, and we were excited about meeting our first placement in just a few weeks' time.

The urge to help children had been building up in me since I was a kid myself. I'd witnessed first-hand what happens to forgotten youngsters behind closed doors, how society deepens their misery either by glossing over their suffering or looking the other way.

And as I stood in that church hall echoing with children's laughter, I couldn't help thinking about other poor kiddies out there who weren't as lucky or as loved as these youngsters.

There were some hidden away, like I had been as a child, and others living among us who were more likely to get a thump than a present on Christmas morning.

The lack of love and compassion I've seen in my lifetime is heart-breaking. Young people, running away from unimaginable violence dished out by the people who are supposed to care for them the most, can fall into the hands of other predators and abusers.

It's kids like these that I'd always wanted to reach out to.

The opportunity to do just that came sooner than I expected.

Arriving home from Stevie's Nativity play, I could hear the telephone ringing as I put the key in door.

It was Carol, the link worker from the foster agency – the person who acted as the liaison between us and social services whenever a new case cropped up.

I hadn't expected to hear from her yet, especially at 8 o'clock on a Monday night just before Christmas.

"Hello Carol, what's up?"

The relief at the other end of the phone was palpable.

"Thank goodness you're there," she said, sounding like the weight of the world was on her shoulders. "I know you weren't expecting to start this just yet, but do you think you could take a child in need now? Before Christmas?" she asked.

I paused for a second, trying to take it in.

"We've got nothing ready at home yet." I hesitated. "You know I wasn't expecting our first child for at least another month."

"I'm so sorry this has come at such short notice, Jeanie," said Carol, "but we have an urgent situation on our hands. We need a temporary foster mum for a baby girl who's just a few days old. I've tried everywhere, but not one of our established families can do it.

Is there any chance at all you could take her in? It would only be a temporary arrangement, at least until an adoptive family is found. Or her mother comes forward."

This would certainly be a delicate first placement. But, I wondered, could we cope with it while we had a houseful – our three boisterous kids and Bill's mum – over the festive season?

My mind was busily trying to remember what babies need and trying to figure out where the baby would sleep. As well as looking after two adults and three children, I'd need to make up bottles of formula milk, change piles of nappies and sort out the baby's bath and night routines.

But honestly, even at that point, I knew what my answer would be. Despite the hard work it would entail, you would have needed a heart of stone to turn away a little mite like that. Her first Christmas, like every child's, should have been with her mum and dad, and yet here she was, alone in the world.

Taking her in wasn't just up to me, though. When you decide to foster, the entire family has to be on board.

"I'd like to say yes," I told Carol, "but I'll have to talk to Bill and the kids first. Does this baby girl really have no other family at all?"

When I started fostering, phone calls from case workers would usually contain minimal information, and we would only learn more about the child's background when the social worker dropped them off at our home.

But because this was an urgent placement and potentially our first, Carol filled me in with more detail.

"I'm afraid we don't know who her family is," she said. "Father Gerry at St Mary Magdalene's found her abandoned in a wicker basket on the steps of his church. Poor thing was wrapped in an old towel and some blankets. As a newborn she was lucky to have survived the night in this weather. But she's a real little fighter, this one."

The abandoned baby girl was being looked after in hospital, but now she was strong enough to be discharged.

"Any sign of the mother at all?" I asked, aware that there was a confused mum out there, probably in need of medical attention and a shoulder to cry on.

I understood only too well how desperate a girl like that could be.

"There was no note with the baby, nothing," Carol sighed. "But one clue to the mum's identity is the red anorak that was draped around the outside of the basket. There's a name tag sewn into the collar with 'Angela' written on it and an age 14 label."

"Probably still at school then," I said, thinking out loud. "That poor girl."

"I think we have to assume that's likely," continued Carol. "After examining the baby, doctors think Angela – if that is the mother's name – must have cut the umbilical cord herself. Which means she obviously didn't give birth in a hospital, so we can't trace her that way.

"Our concern is that she could well have contracted a serious infection, and unless she comes forward or we find her, her life may be in danger."

An array of disturbing memories from my own teenage years flashed through my mind. I knew exactly what this young mum Angela was going through, and my heart ached for her.

Carol continued. "Oh, because of the time of year, the nurses have named her Holly…"

I was in a bit of daze as I wandered into the front room to tell Bill. He knew from my expression that something serious was afoot.

"Whatever's happened?" he asked.

"Carol at the agency has asked if we can look after a baby over Christmas," I said, trying to read his face for a reaction. "There's no other foster family available."

"Well that's a bolt from the blue," he exclaimed, brushing his hand over his forehead.

To my relief, he started to smile.

"Shall we talk it over with the rest of the team, then?" he said.

With that, I sat everyone around the big pine table in the kitchen while Bill warmed a pan of milk to make hot chocolate.

"What do you all think about welcoming a baby girl this Christmas, kids?" I asked, trying to sound neutral as I spooned cocoa powder into mugs.

Although we had already talked about fostering children, it was important not to make them feel under pressure to do so now, over Christmas and at short notice. If they didn't really want to do it, resentment would set in and we would all regret it later.

"Tell us if you think it's too soon," I began, "but do you feel ready to have a baby girl at home with us right away? Her name is Holly and she's only a few days old. So that will mean me making up bottles, changing nappies, and yes, there will be crying during the night. It's what babies do, you see."

Stevie wrinkled his nose at the mention of "nappies".

"That's ok, Stevie. If any of you think it's too much over Christmas, that's absolutely fine," I said calmly. "It's important that we're all honest and express how we really feel."

Quietly sipping their drinks, our three kids thought for a moment, evidently as surprised as we were to be presented with this dilemma.

"I'm happy with it!" exclaimed 10-year-old Sophie. "Holly can have all my old baby clothes. And my nursery set."

"Well, I don't think she's quite ready to use cutlery yet, love, but that's a very kind offer," I said with a smile. "And I'm sure your little pink booties and bonnet Nana Ivy knitted for you will look lovely on her."

Sophie bounded off upstairs to search through the old chest in my bedroom where I still kept some of the kids' baby clothes.

Within no time she was pattering back through the hallway, proudly holding the pastel matinee sets knitted for her and Stevie by Bill's mum, her Nana Ivy.

"Mum, I'll help you look after baby Holly," my oldest daughter Sarah declared earnestly. "Even in the middle of the night."

It struck me with alarm how close in age Sarah was to baby Holly's teenage mum and I shuddered at the thought of my 13-year-old girl being in the same predicament.

"Don't worry, love," I said. "You can leave the night feeds and the crying to me. But any other help, like a nice cup of tea and a plate of biscuits once in a while, would be most welcome!"

Despite his outburst over the dirty nappies, Stevie seemed happy enough, too.

"Holly can come here, as long as she doesn't scream *all* night," he said, licking the chocolate froth from the back of his spoon. "Or take my Lego," he added firmly as an afterthought.

Sarah giggled at the ludicrous notion of a tiny baby wanting to play with Stevie's toys.

Discussion over, they charged upstairs to get ready for bed. The sound of thuds and squeals as they raced to the top defused the tension over what we had to decide overnight.

"Just down to you and me now, love," I said to Bill.

We looked at one another, trying to gauge what the other was thinking.

"You go first," I said.

"Well, it's been sprung on us when we were least expecting it," Bill said cautiously. "And we haven't got much time to prepare at all, especially for a newborn baby…"

My head knew he was right, but my heart was telling me something quite different. And thankfully so was his.

"But so what, let's go for it," he smiled. "One more small person around the table at Christmas won't make any difference. There's plenty of room at the inn."

I knew deep down that we were doing the right thing. It's the reason we wanted to foster in the first place, to help kids in desperate situations.

Not only that, but it was exciting, too, the thought of having a baby in the house again.

First thing the next morning I called Carol with the good news.

"Our answer is yes," I said. "We've all talked about it and we would love to welcome Holly into our home."

"Jeanie, that's fantastic," Carol replied with an audible sigh of relief.

"So when do we get to meet her?" I asked.

"How about this Saturday? I can bring her over in the afternoon with Janet, the social worker."

"Perfect," I replied, not missing a beat. "Just let me know what we need to prepare for her in advance."

"Well, she came to us with nothing except that red anorak, although the hospital did find her a couple of sleep-suits," Carol said, before reeling off a quick list. "If you have any snug onesies, some warm blankets and woolly hats, that would be perfect. Oh, and a cot. Do you have one?"

"I'll have to get back to you about that," I replied.

While the baby clothes were already taken care of, I wasn't sure where, with only three days before Holly's arrival, we would find a cot.

"No problem," said Bill. "We've already got one. The kids' old cot is in the attic. I dismantled it after Stevie moved into his bunk. With a bit of a clean-up and an MOT, it will be as good as new."

I knew I could always rely on my calm, purposeful and practical Bill to look on the bright side. Whenever there was a problem to solve, he was my rock.

"Thanks, love," I said, reaching up to give him a kiss.

"While you're sorting the cot, I'd better go and buy some new baby bottles and formula milk – and practise how to make it. It's been a long time since I've bottle-fed a baby."

The Boy Across the Street

Ever since I was little, I've loved children. With an instinctive urge to mother everyone, I used to look out for the youngsters down the Dublin street where I was brought up and, later, the older girls at my convent school.

"You're a born mother," my own mum would tell me whenever she saw me clucking over the little ones.

I loved wrapping them in a hand-knitted blanket, putting them in our tattered old buggy and pushing them up and down the cobbled pavement outside our terraced house.

The youngest of five kids, I lived with my family in a two-up two-down in one of those working-class areas where everyone knew each other's business.

As a family of seven, there wasn't much space in our little end of terrace. Mum and Dad's room was the largest, of course, which wasn't saying much, and my four older brothers somehow managed to pile into the back bedroom, topping and tailing like sardines on a bed with a horse-hair mattress.

My little room – a tiny garret with a sloping ceiling up in the attic – was accessed by a narrow wooden staircase. There were always a few cobwebs festooning the dark corners, and hardly any light shone through the miniscule window in the eaves, but I loved my snug little room at the top of the house, I felt safe there.

When I think about my childhood, I felt loved above all. Those were the days when you could leave your doors unlocked, play carefree out in the streets and rely on a neighbour to help whenever you needed it. We didn't have much, but we had affection and food on the table, and that was enough.

I suppose we were what could be described as content – happy even, despite the poverty that put everyone in my close-knit community in the same boat.

Not every family, however, was as fortunate as ours.

Struggling to survive had a destructive effect on some, and even as a child I became aware that when the head of a family tried to drown his sorrows in alcohol, it was often his wife and kids who suffered. And not just because he spent all his earnings on booze.

Drunkenness and violence often went hand in hand, and domestic abuse behind closed doors was as much a fact of life then as it is now.

My calling to become a foster mother years later may have been prompted by what I witnessed at a young age and led to my urge to protect innocent victims.

I'll never forget Johnny, the boy who lived across the street. When he and his family moved into the house opposite, a dreadful shadow fell over us.

Peering through the little window in my attic room, I could see most of what was going on around us – and I didn't like what was happening in his house one bit.

The first time I saw Johnny's drunken dad hit him, I gasped and recoiled in horror. With the full force of his spade-like hands, he whacked his son around the head, not once but several times, almost knocking the poor kid over.

When Johnny's mum tried to throw herself between them, to shield her boy, she copped a thump, too.

I watched in disbelief, shaking with fear at the thought of how far this brute of a man would go next time. And there were plenty of next times.

After these vicious attacks, Johnny would walk slowly to school with his head bowed, wearing a cap to try and hide the angry bruises and red finger marks across his cheeks.

"What's that on your face, Johnny?" a teacher asked loudly, sounding more accusatory than concerned.

"I bumped it, miss," he muttered, avoiding her gaze.

He had retreated into himself, consumed by sadness and shame.

"Isn't she going to do anything to help him?" I thought, horrified by her indifference.

But no, she just carried on marking the pile of books on her desk with her red pen.

She knew what was happening – the whole school did – but no-one could be bothered to put their head above the parapet to protect kids like Johnny. In those days, there was no real recourse for domestic abuse and kids were considered fair game.

I was lucky that my parents were different. Throughout my childhood they never once laid a hand on me or my brothers, even when we were naughty.

So it was my mission to help Johnny, the boy across the street.

"Can he come and stay with us?" I asked Mum as she worked her way through a big pile of washing in the galvanised metal tub in our small scullery.

With sheets, blankets and clothes from the seven of us sitting in a huge heap on the cold tiled floor, there was a lot to get through. Mum, who worked herself ragged keeping the house spotless, did all the washing by hand, just like all the other women in our neighbourhood.

The day I approached her with my unusual request, she looked exhausted again. The shadows under her eyes seemed darker than ever against her pallid complexion, and her glossy jet-black hair – once her pride and joy – had lost its lustre.

She stopped mopping the steam from her brow and turned around.

"Whatever for, Jeanie?" she replied, frowning in bewilderment.

These were the days when children wouldn't have dreamed of asking for sleepovers at their friends' homes.

With multiple siblings often sharing the same bedroom, inviting another youngster to stay the night just wasn't the done thing in working-class families like ours.

"We don't really know him," Mum continued, "and I don't think his mam and dad would let him come here even if we did."

"But his dad doesn't like him," I said flatly.

"How do you know that, Jeanie?" she asked, surprise rising in her voice.

"He hurts him, Mam," I stammered. "A lot…"

In hushed tones, because what I had seen Johnny's dad do was so awful, I described to her what I had witnessed from my room.

"That's terrible," she replied softly, shaking her head in dismay. "I'll tell your dad, see if he can have a word."

I imagined my dad striding across the street and banging on the door. Would Johnny's mum appear, wiping her hands on her pinny, before calling to her husband? I imagined the monster emerging, his big burly frame filling the doorway, fists clenched ready to strike. But then I pictured my kind gentle Dad standing his ground and warning, "If you lay a hand on Johnny again, you'll have someone your own size to deal with." My dad, the hero. I hoped he wasn't going to get hurt because of me.

But that's not what happened at all. After Dad came home from his shift, I heard muffled voices from downstairs, then his voice raised in anger.

"I've told you, it's none of our business how a man chooses to run his family," he stormed at my mum. "Now, I don't want to hear another word about it."

He came up to my room later and asked me if I wanted to help him lay the table for tea. He never laid the table – for tea or any other meal. "No thanks," I said, barely able to look at him. He sat at the end of my bed, his face looking all upset, like when he had to tell me that next door's dog had died.

"Look Jeanie, I know you want to help your friend but there's nothing I can do. It might even make it worse if I interfere," he said gently.

"But who will help Johnny if we don't?" I asked, tears stinging my eyes.

"You can't always help, Jeanie, even if you want to," said Dad.

I think I instinctively knew then what I surely know now: the important thing is to try. Johnny and his family moved up to Connemara a few weeks later and I never saw him again.

After the Johnny drama, my family was knocked for six by a tragedy of our own. When I was only 10 years old my mum was diagnosed with breast cancer.

The kind of woman who would never admit she was ill, Mum would get up and continue with her chores as usual no matter how poorly she felt. She'd brush aside coughs and colds, waking up at 5am as regular as clockwork every day to light the fire and make our porridge. Languishing in bed, she would say, was sheer laziness and a selfish luxury.

She was the engine that kept our family going and such a strong force that we had no idea she was unwell.

With a family of seven to clothe, cook and clean for, she often looked tired and pale. But then the shadows under her eyes got darker, her naturally fair complexion started to look washed out and by tea time she would fall asleep, exhausted, in her chair by the fire.

"Are you all right, Mary?" my Dad once asked, frowning in concern as he touched her trembling hand.

"I'm as right as rain, Patrick," she'd replied curtly, suddenly getting up to busy herself with a tea towel at the sink. "Don't fuss, now."

Like a lot of women of her stalwart generation, she was of the opinion that you "just get on with it" when life pulls the rug from underneath you.

Believing she was made of sterner stuff, she tried to hide from us the fact that she was feeling poorly. But eventually she wasn't able to pretend any longer.

"I'm so sorry," she said, fighting back tears after Dad found her unconscious on the ground in our back yard. "I felt dizzy and tripped, that's all. That flagstone is a bit slippery.

"But I'll be fine," she continued, placing her hand over the cut on her forehead and tugging down the hem of her skirt to conceal the bloody gash on her knee. "I just need a sit down with a hot cup of sweet tea and I'll be right as rain."

Mum had collapsed while pegging out yet another load of washing. In those days you had to gather water by hand from a pump outside, boil it up in a pan, fill the dolly tub, then wash and rinse the clothes by hand, before putting them through a mangle to squeeze off the excess water.

Compared to the ease of loading dirty clothes into a washing machine and simply pressing a switch, the weekly washing that always took place on a Monday when I was a kid was like hard labour.

But it wasn't the strain of looking after a big family that had made Mum keel over. It was something far more sinister than that.

Dad was unconvinced by Mum's insistence that she was fine. He called out the local doctor who, after examining her, drove her straight to hospital.

He'd found a lump on her breast, which she told him she thought was "nothing and would go away by itself..."

It was then that the devastating diagnosis was made. Mum's cancer was too advanced for any treatment to be effective. There was no chemotherapy in those days, just radiation and surgery, but both these options were too late for Mum.

She died four months later, in her bed at home, with Dad and all of us children around her. She was only 36 years old.

The loss of Mum felt like an aching chasm. Without her steady, gentle presence running the home, quietly steering the ship, it was as if the very soul had been ripped out of our lives.

Grief-stricken, Dad buried himself in his work, taking on even more shifts down the docks, partly to make more money to look after us, but also so that he didn't have to face coming back to a house without the woman he'd loved so steadfastly.

Despite help from a few relatives and kind neighbours who brought over meals during the weeks following Mum's death, he struggled to look after five kids on his own.

"We'll manage, we're a team," he'd insist, vowing to keep us together against all the odds.

But then the burden of harsh reality set in.

Week after relentless week, there were five hungry mouths to cook for, washing to be done and a house to run, and only poor Dad to do it all.

Eventually the challenge of caring for us, providing comfort after Mum's death and keeping a roof over our heads, proved too much for him.

While two of my brothers were old enough to leave school and get work at the docks with Dad, the younger two were taken in by an aunt and uncle who, with no children of their own, were glad of a couple of lads to train up to work down on their farm in Wicklow.

That left me, the youngest, and the only girl.

As my secure, happy world shattered, I withdrew into my shell. The thought of leaving Dad, of losing him from my life, gave me nightmares.

So, in my childlike way, I tried to make sure it never happened.

I'd make us breakfast – usually burning the toast – and get myself ready for school. When I came home in the afternoon, I'd shut myself in my room and read, escaping into a fantasy world through my books, until Dad and my brothers had finished their shifts.

Weary from a long day's toil, Dad would move sluggishly around the kitchen, trying to cobble together a meal for us all, before slumping in exhaustion in his armchair – the only place he would sleep after Mum died, because he couldn't face going back into their room.

He found it increasingly hard to cope. Slogging through a 12-hour shift while trying to keep a home going was proving to be impossible.

A staunch Catholic all his life, Dad turned to the church in the midst of his grief, hoping his faith would help heal his broken heart.

One Sunday after Mass, our elderly priest Father Joseph took him to one side.

"Jeanie could board at St Hilda's," he said in his soft Irish lilt, peering benevolently at me over his wire-rimmed glasses.

Clinging to Dad's arm, I recoiled in dismay at the thought of living away from home in a cold, draughty convent.

It was an instinct that later proved to be well founded, and not just because of the cold.

"There will be many young girls in similar situations to you, Jeanie," Father Joseph continued, noting my fear as he tried to reassure me with his soothing tones. "You'll make lots of new friends. Now wouldn't that be nice?"

"Jeanie would be well looked after by the Sisters," he added, seeing my dad's uncertainty.

"Would I be allowed to visit her, Father?" Dad's voice was quiet and choked with emotion as he fidgeted nervously with his old, frayed leather-bound Bible. "And would she come home for the holidays?"

Father Joseph nodded solemnly. "I'll speak to the Mother Superior," he said, tenderly placing a hand on Dad's shoulder. "You and Jeanie can meet her at the convent and we'll see how it goes, shall we?"

I suddenly felt numb. Trembling, I stared at the ancient stone slabs of the church floor, trying not to cry in front of Father Joseph, who Dad held in such high reverence and who seemed to be doing our family an almighty good service.

But on the bus going home, the floodgates opened and my body shook with the despairing sobs I couldn't hold in. I'd already lost my mam, I couldn't bear the thought of losing him too.

"I don't want to leave you, Daddy," I cried, burying my face in the lapel of his Sunday-best tweed jacket, which had started to smell of whiskey and tobacco.

I knew that Dad had secretly taken up smoking – and drinking – again after Mum died.

"Don't worry, pet," he said, wrapping his arms around me. "I'll visit you whenever I can. And you'll be home for the holidays. Just think of all the new friends you'll make, lots of little girls like you."

But his heart was breaking, too. Sending me away into the care of the nuns wasn't what he wanted, but he could see no way out. With his deep faith in the church and those who claimed to serve it, he really believed it was in my best interests.

In reality it turned out to be one of the worst experiences of my life. It felt like a six-year sentence of mindless punishment, willful neglect and shocking brutality, all behind closed doors and in the name of God – who, I never believed for one moment, would have advocated such viciousness.

"Why doesn't God intervene?" I used to wonder. "Surely he wouldn't let cruelty like this continue?"

But perhaps he guided me to help prevent the continued abuse of other children. If you believe, as I do, in a reason for everything, my experience at the convent school could have been the catalyst for my future career as a foster mum.

Twisted Sisters

Since fostering over a hundred youngsters, I am only too aware of the evils lurking in wait for them. My own experience at St Hilda's taught me that abuse, violence and neglect can lie hidden in plain sight, carried out by the very people who are meant to be nurturing a child.

Sister Gertrude was the cruellest nun in the convent and, looking back on it, probably not the full shilling. She had a gammy leg that caused her pain and she would limp around the corridors searching for some unlucky kid to take it out on.

In a bid at retaliation, we nicknamed her "Gertrude the Gorgon" after the mythological creature that could turn you to stone with just one look.

There were many times when I witnessed Sister Gertrude thrashing some poor girl over a minor misdemeanour. I've never been one to look away and when I entreated her to stop – as I often did – the sadistic nun would simply turn on me instead.

"Watch your tongue, girl!" she'd hiss, her cold grey eyes flashing through her pebble-thick glasses. "And stop gawping. Who do you think you are? You're nothing special."

In a frenzy, the embittered old battle-axe would lift her hand – or a ruler, wooden sandal, even a Bible – high in the air and repeatedly whack it into my body.

As much as her relentless blows hurt, I'd bite my lip and dig my nails into the palms of my hands to stop myself from crying.

She and her coven of black-robed crones wanted to break us, to squeeze any spirit or sense of worth out of us, but I wouldn't be crushed.

"You *will* cry," they'd sneer, whipping us with their leather belts and canes, or whatever came to hand. "Pride is a sin."

If you so much as sneezed in church, fainted from hunger or forgot one of your times-tables, you'd be slapped, punched or have your hair pulled. Physical punishment for the tiniest transgression was an accepted part of the culture at this convent.

Heaven help you if you wet the bed…

"You wicked girl!" Sister Gertrude spat in fury. She forced Mabel, one of the petrified girls in my dormitory, to stand all night with the dripping-wet sheets draped over her shivering body.

That poor girl must have caught pneumonia. She went down with a fever and we never saw her again.

"Where's Mabel?" I dared to ask Sister Bernadette, one of the kinder, younger nuns.

"She's gone home, child," she whispered, her eyes fearfully darting around in case Sister Gertrude was arriving to do one of her infamous spot inspections.

"But Mabel doesn't have a home," I said. "She's an orphan."

Whatever really happened to the poor girl, it was all hushed up and even I knew better than to push for more information.

As so-called pillars of the community, these tyrant nuns could get away with unspeakable brutality behind closed doors while presenting a virtuous façade to the world outside.

Whenever Dad and the other parents visited us, Sister Gertrude transformed herself into charm personified. She was all smiles, tea and cake as she put on a warped show of hideous hypocrisy.

"Tell Dad what's going on," an inner voice told me as I sat with him in the convent's dining hall, talking to him about my lessons and why Sister Gertrude had complained to him that I needed to try harder at Religious Instruction.

It was on the tip of my tongue on so many occasions, but like suspicious prison guards, the Gorgon and her cohort of informers were never far away, loitering behind us to listen to our conversations in case somebody grassed them up.

"What is it, Jeanie?" Dad asked. "You look a bit tired and pale." I was on the verge of telling him how worried I was about Mabel, the girl who had suddenly disappeared.

"Oh, … it's nothing," I managed to stutter. "There was a girl here that left and I wondered what had happened to her, that's all."

Whenever I looked at Dad's haggard face, my courage to go any further deserted me. He had enough on his plate after Mum died and could do without having to deal with this mess, too. Instead, I would shield him from the horror of it all.

"Everything's fine, Dad," I lied. "How are my brothers?"

But it wasn't just Dad I was trying to protect. It was a case of self-preservation, too.

"If you tell him," a voice within me warned, "Sister Gertrude will thrash you to within an inch of your life. It will be your word against hers."

Like most controlling abusers, she and her sidekicks knew how to silence us. They had created an atmosphere of constant terror. When one girl broke out and legged it to the nearest police station to tell them what was happening, the garda phoned the convent to come and pick her up.

These policemen had been brought up to believe that the idea of sacred nuns using violence was unthinkable, and that this girl was maligning them.

She certainly paid the price for her bravery. Locked in solitary confinement, she was fed on only dry bread and water for a week.

"To starve the devil out of you," as Sister Gertrude put it.

There was no energy or fight left in her when she emerged, weak and thin, from her locked room, and that was exactly how the Sisters wanted it.

"If you talk about this, you'll never see your parents again," was their chilling threat to the rest of us. And we believed them, as children are programmed to do with adults in authority.

There were a few nuns at the convent who made our lives just about bearable. New to its savage regime, they were too timid and afraid to challenge the older guard.

They'd speak gently to us when the other nuns weren't within earshot, and one in particular – Sister Winifred – would smile and surreptitiously pop dolly mixtures into our hands if we were good in class.

"Here you go, sweetie," she'd say, her soft Irish lilt a balm to our bruised souls.

She would have been in big trouble if Sister Gertrude had caught her being nice; that old witch seemed to enjoy dishing out punishment to the younger nuns almost as much as she did terrorising us.

"Out of my way, you eejits!" she'd screech as they scattered in her wake, the back of her hand clipping whoever was unfortunate enough to be in her path.

If there's one thing my school days at the convent taught me, it is the appalling, long-lasting impact of physical and emotional abuse.

The injustice of it all filled me with a sense of rage that I feel to this day and was one of the driving forces behind why I wanted to be a foster mum in the first place.

I recalled the forlorn youngsters at the convent, whose teenage mothers had been forced – or were willing – to give them up as babies because they had been conceived outside of marriage.

The lucky ones had been adopted by caring families, but the most unfortunate children had ended up being entrusted to the cold, cruel care of Sister Gertrude and her coven of heartless harpies.

I saw first-hand how some of the nuns would unjustly punish the child for what they described as "the sins of the mother," forever telling them that they were worthless and should be grateful for the privilege of being swept up into their holy enclave.

"Wicked old bats," I murmured under my breath. "You're the ones who should feel shame. Every child is born innocent."

Although Sister Gertrude and her mob didn't cause me to reject religion or my belief in God, I still shiver at my memories of that bleak period of my life.

To this day, whenever I see a nun in a black habit, I experience a knee-jerk reaction. I have to stop to catch my breath and feel physically sick at the memories it stirs up.

I would never forget this unholy communion of silence and abuse. Years later, I used those feelings to fuel my mission to help other kids who had experienced such appalling brutality.

Pregnant Teen

After my experience at the convent, I vowed that when I had my own children I would never let anyone take them from me. I'd fight like a lioness defending her cubs if anyone tried to lay even so much as a finger on them.

But then, becoming a mum happened far sooner than I had expected – and certainly not in the way I would have wished.

After leaving the convent at 16, I returned home to live with Dad, who had become frail and aged beyond his years since Mum died.

Despite my fiery nature, I was an innocent when it came to men and very naive sexually, which made me an easy target for one unscrupulous so-called pillar of the community. He was a friend of Dad's and he forced himself on me one Sunday when we were walking back on our own from Mass. I didn't tell a soul. I couldn't. Not about the rape, nor when I discovered to my horror that I was expecting a baby.

In those days in Ireland, a woman who got pregnant out of wedlock was considered to be no better than a whore, especially in the Catholic community where I grew up.

Nobody cared much about the detail of how you came to be pregnant in the first place. No matter that you had been pressured into having sex, molested and coerced by an older man, or had even been raped: it was considered to be your fault for bringing shame on yourself and your family – and you had to suffer the consequences. While the boys and men who put you in the family way got off scot-free, you were deemed to be tainted, soiled goods. It wasn't fair, but that's just the way it was. An unmarried pregnant girl was "a wicked girl who was no better than she should be."

There was no question of me not having the baby: abortion was a mortal sin, and illegal, too, so it was not something I would even consider. But as a pregnant single teenager, I knew I wouldn't be the only one to suffer condemnation. Whatever the rights and wrongs of my situation, I couldn't bear to bring shame on my family, and would never allow anyone to take my baby away.

So I decided to go into self-imposed exile. By making a new life for myself in England, I figured, strangers would know nothing of my past.

"I'll pretend that I'm married but my husband deserted me," I said to myself. "No one needs to know the truth." I would wear Mum's engagement ring on my wedding finger and turn round the tiny diamond so that it looked like a simple gold band.

Innocently, or naively, I thought I had it all worked out.

When I started to suffer from morning sickness, I told Dad I'd eaten something that didn't agree with me. It wouldn't have crossed his mind that his daughter was pregnant. As far as Dad was concerned, I would be a virgin on my wedding day, like Mum had been with him.

In a state of confusion and denial, I didn't take positive action until I was five months gone and struggling to hide my growing bump beneath the baggy smock tops that, luckily, were fashionable at the time.

Through a friend I'd made at the convent, I heard that there were machinist jobs going at a factory in Lancashire, England. This was my chance.

I loathed lying to Dad, but the alternative – bringing down his reputation in our staunch Roman Catholic community – seemed far worse to me.

Becoming a machinist in a busy city like Salford, a place large enough to swallow me up and let me go about my business in anonymity, seemed like the perfect answer to my predicament.

I didn't even think about how I would cope in a job with a baby on the way, let alone look after it on my own once it was born.

Naively I figured that if I could earn a wage as a machinist, making clothes in one of the mills after my baby was born, it would all slot into place.

Ever since I was little, I had enjoyed sewing. I was enthralled by the colours of the thread and the soft sound it made as the needle slid through the fabric.

Mum used to make my little dresses by hand from old curtains until Dad bought her a second-hand manual sewing machine to make her life easier. When she showed me how to stitch clothes for my teddies and dolls, there was no stopping me.

I cherished our visits to the little wool shop on the corner, where reels of shiny cotton and skeins of thread and wool were all laid out in such tempting displays.

Later, I would sit in our back room with Mum, making a jacket for my teddy while her sewing machine whirred away on a new pair of curtains, trousers for the boys, or a dress for me.

I would often look up from my work, completely fascinated and full of admiration for her skill and the finely tailored garments she created out of next to nothing. She would have made a top-notch seamstress if she had been given the chance.

After she died, I had taught myself how to use her old Singer. Sitting on her stool at her little work table, I practised on scraps of material from discarded clothes.

Recalling how she'd dexterously turn the fabric, I repeated her nifty manoeuvres and within a few weeks felt confident and capable enough to run up a patchwork quilt for Dad, curtains for the parlour, and a skirt for myself.

But now, as a pregnant, soon-to-be teenage mum, my skirts were bursting at the seams.

I had never been a skinny girl – delicious Irish stews, bacon and cabbage dinners, soda bread and apple puddings put paid to that. But even as a rather curvy young woman, my bump was growing at such a rate that before long I would no longer be able to hide it.

However, my Dad was not convinced by my sudden plans to leave Ireland on my own.

"Stop playing the maggot, Jeanie; you've never lived away from home before," he said doubtfully. "Except for when you were at the convent, and that doesn't count because you were protected there. It's not safe for a young girl in England. There are folk... men who would take advantage."

I resisted the urge to laugh bitterly at the irony.

"Dad, I would hardly describe the convent as a place of protection," I retorted.

Spinning around to look straight at me, his bright blue eyes flashed anger and shock.

"You were looked after by the good Sisters there. They were like mothers to you!"

"They weren't anything like a mother – mine or anyone else's!"

"What do you mean?" he yelled. "The nuns kept you safe. You should be grateful, my girl!"

I bit my lip. "Oh Dad, if only you knew the truth," I wanted to yell back. "*They* were the ones I needed protecting from!"

But when I saw his crestfallen expression, his exhausted, grief-stricken body crumple in front of me, I didn't have the heart to tell him.

What good would it have done, destroying all that Dad held sacred and dear? Then, on top of all that, telling him I was pregnant? How could I tell him that I didn't need to travel to England to be taken advantage of: it had already happened right under his nose, in our own town and at the hands of his so-called friend?

It would kill what was left of him, damage his soul and make him blame himself.

No, I would shoulder the burden of this mess and work out how I would tell him about the baby later.

"I'm sorry, Dad," I said, my voice soft and soothing now as I put my arms around him. "There's not much work for me here, and this job is a real opportunity.

"Besides, you don't want me under your feet forever," I continued, choking back tears. "I've just turned 18, I'm a grown up. I'm spreading my wings, just like you did when you were my age. I'll be in a busy city, using a skill that Mum taught me. I want to make you both proud."

That last part stuck in my throat, but I convinced myself that it was only a little white lie. And the mention of mum always softened my dad.

"Do you have a place to live, Jeanie?" he asked with a sigh of resignation.

"Yes, of course, Dad," I said casually, careful to avoid eye contact that might give me away. "I'll stay in a boarding house with Aileen, my friend from the convent. We'll have a landlady, who I've heard is a bit of a dragon, so she'll keep all the boys away."

I noted inwardly and with shame that I had become quite the accomplished liar, and each lie that tripped from my lips made me feel as if I had swallowed a cold, hard stone.

"We've been offered a cosy little room to share," I continued, swallowing a lie the size of a boulder with my non-existent chaste arrangements. "A few of the factory girls board there, too."

None of this was true, of course, but I convinced myself that before long it would be. That's when I would put everything right and it would all work out – me, the baby, Dad, my family.

"Promise me, Jeanie, that you'll write to me every week and tell me all your news," Dad insisted. "I'll need to know you're safe and happy over there. It's not like here, you know, you won't be able to trust too many people in a city like that."

"I promise," I whispered with a feeble nod.

Reaching into his pocket, Dad pulled out his old leather wallet and as he opened it up, I glimpsed the faded sepia picture of Mum on their wedding day that he carried with him everywhere. Beaming at the camera, her raven hair framing her porcelain complexion and tumbling in waves over the white lace wedding dress she had made herself, she looked so young, so beautiful, so full of hope for the future.

Tears pricked my eyes as I remembered how, just before she was diagnosed with cancer, she had proudly shown me this exquisite gown.

I had sat mesmerised on her bed as she lifted a powder-blue box from the back of her wardrobe. With great reverence, she unfolded the yellowed tissue paper to reveal her precious, pristine white gown.

There was just a hint of sadness in her eyes as she held it up against herself in front of the mirror on her dressing table and gazed wistfully at her reflection. Her face was pale and care-worn now, her black hair streaked with grey, but to me my mother would always be beautiful.

Seeing my expression in the mirror as I watched her, Mum said, "This dress will be yours one day, Jeanie. It'll be my gift to you on your wedding day. You'll be a beautiful bride, my love, to be sure."

I hadn't understood it at the time, but looking back at that tender scene, the penny suddenly dropped with a force that took my breath away: Mum had already known she wouldn't be there to watch me walk down the aisle. She must have already found the lump in her breast and understood what it meant. Knowing that she wouldn't live long enough to see me wed must have broken her heart.

A coldness crept through my veins as a familiar voice screeched out its poison in my head.

"You, wearing white on your wedding day?" sneered Sister Gertrude in the shrill rasp that would haunt me for the rest of my life. "You're nothing but a harlot carrying a bastard child. No man would stoop to marry you, you wicked girl!"

The voice in my head was right about one thing: I wasn't worthy enough to wear Mum's white wedding dress. I'd lied to Dad and let them both down.

As I stood there trembling with shame and sadness, two warm hands reached out and touched mine.

"Here you go, pet," said Dad, pressing a wad of pound notes – his last lot of wages plus overtime – into my hand.

"If I don't hear from you once a week, me and your brothers will be on the next boat over and come looking for you," he added, forcing a smile.

"Thanks, Dad," I whispered. "I won't waste it."

"I know that, Jeanie," he said, then handed me an envelope. "This is to keep you safe."

Inside was a photo of Mum, serene and smiling in her best blue dress with me as a babe in arms.

"Oh Dad…" I couldn't speak. My lovely mum, the person I now needed more than anyone in the world. How I missed her gentle wisdom.

There was also something shiny rustling inside the envelope: Mum's silver St Christopher.

"Your grandmother gave your mum this necklace for her First Holy Communion and she was saving it for her first grandchild," said Dad, oblivious to the torment his words brought. "But I want you to have it now, Jeanie. Keep it with you and Mum will always be looking over you."

With a heavy heart, I packed a small suitcase ready for the early ferry from Dublin the next morning. Dad offered to come and see me off, but we both knew it was best that he didn't. Neither of us wanted a long, drawn-out goodbye, both of us smiling brightly and pretending our hearts weren't breaking. I couldn't bear the thought of seeing him on the quayside, waving steadfastly at the departing boat until he was just a smudge on the horizon.

I hugged him before I went up to bed, the next day's journey hanging heavily between us. "You look after yourself, Dad," I whispered into his neck.

"Write to me when you get there," he said gruffly. "And let me know if you need any money."

I slipped out of the house just after dawn, before anyone was up. As I boarded the boat, I had never felt so totally alone. The Irish Sea was wild that day. I wandered around the ferry deck like a lost soul, feeling sick throughout the turbulent crossing into the unknown.

Guardian Angel

Leaving behind the country I loved was traumatic enough, but trying to find a place to live in Salford as an unmarried pregnant woman was a nightmare. How deluded was I to think I could survive on my own?

It was the year before the Race Relations Act of 1968 and I was horrified to see hostile signs in windows stating, "No Coloureds, No Irish, No Dogs, No Children."

With a sinking feeling I realised that I already ticked two of the boxes on this vile list. Before my feet had touched the ground I already knew my place and it was in the gutter.

Trudging the streets, looking for a place to stay, I rotated Mum's engagement ring on the second finger of my left hand to make it look as if I was a respectable married woman.

But the rules were slightly different here. People seemed more concerned that I was Irish and pregnant rather than worrying whether or not I had tied the knot before committing the "sin" of conceiving a child.

Door after door was slammed in my face as soon as the sour-faced landladies heard my southern Irish accent or clocked my burgeoning bump. Although I had enough money to stay in a boarding house, they wouldn't let me set foot over the threshold.

It pains me to recall that I had no choice but to sleep rough.

For the first few nights it bucketed down, so I huddled in shop doorways while people hurrying past in their warm coats and sheltering under their umbrellas shot me glances of disgust.

I was just a lowlife to them.

To maintain some vestige of hygiene, I'd wash my hands and face in public toilets, and using the money Dad gave me, I'd take refuge in working men's cafes, ravenously devouring plates of egg and chips and making a cup of tea last for hours as I watched the world go by through the steamed-up windows.

One day, as I trudged through the hostile red-brick streets, not knowing which way to turn next, I stumbled across a Catholic church.

I smiled when I saw its name. It was called St Mary's – my mother's name – and as I touched her St Christopher around my neck, I wondered if Dad was right, that she really was watching over me. It was a fanciful thought, I know, but it brought me comfort anyway.

Despite my harrowing experience at the convent, my faith hadn't diminished. As I walked down the nave, my footsteps echoing softly, and stood before the statue of Our Lady, I felt as if I had finally found sanctuary. Here was a place where I would, at last, be welcome.

There wasn't a soul in sight, so I sat on the end of a wooden pew near the altar and prayed in the peaceful silence. Despair welled up inside me as I finally acknowledged the hopelessness of my situation. I had no idea where I would go, who I could turn to, or what would become of me and my unborn child.

I was too busy weeping to hear anyone approach.

Suddenly, a hand touched my shoulder.

"There there, love," came a woman's voice. "Whatever's the matter, pet?"

I turned around to see a middle-aged woman in a brown coat and with a broom in her hand. A flowery headscarf framed her plump face and behind her severe glasses, her blue eyes were expressive and kind.

"Sorry," I whispered, self-consciously drying my eyes. "I didn't realise anyone else was here."

"No need to apologise," she soothed, passing me a white cotton hankie with an embroidered initial N, just like the ones my mum always used. "I was just sweeping the vestry when I saw you come in. You looked like you were carrying the weight of the world on your shoulders. I couldn't walk off and leave you like that.

"My lass was your age once; it's a confusing time, isn't it, being a teenage girl?"

I nodded despondently.

"Boyfriend trouble?" she asked.

I shook my head. Weak from sadness and hunger, I trembled and swayed as I attempted to stand up.

Then, grabbing the side of the pew, I murmured, "But yes… I am in trouble."

She glanced at my tummy. "Have you told your mam yet, love?" she asked, gently coaxing me to sit down.

"Mam's not here," I said, choking back another sob. "She died when I was 10. And Dad's back home in Dublin. He has no idea and I couldn't tell him. We're Catholic, you see. So I came here."

"What about the father?" she asked. "Where's he?"

Biting my lip, I stared at the floor and shook my head.

"He… he wants nothing to do with me, with us," I stammered. "I can't… "

There was no judgment in her face as she waited for me to carry on.

"It only happened once and I didn't want it," I said, feeling a huge sense of relief that I had finally been able to tell someone. "He forced himself on me. It's best he's not involved. He's married and everyone will blame me."

For months I'd kept my shameful secret, but now, in the silent shadows of that church, I had confided part of it to a stranger.

Like a guardian angel, Norma was in the right place at the right time for me.

"Where are you living, love?" she asked gently.

"I'm still looking for somewhere," I replied. "Nobody wants me, even though I have the money for rent. They hear my accent, then take one look at my belly and send me packing."

Norma shook her head in disbelief.

"And they call themselves Christians," she said. "I see them at church every Sunday, looking all holier than thou and sucking up to the priest. Hyprocrites, the lot of them."

For the first time since my arrival in England, I felt like I had an ally. Norma was on my side.

After pausing for a few seconds, she looked at me and said, "It's not much, but I have a room where you can stay…"

Seeing a flicker of relief in my eyes, she continued, "It's warm and cosy, and you'll be safe. A young girl in your condition shouldn't be out on the streets. We'll need to get you to a doctor, too."

I knew instinctively I could trust Norma, the only kind person I had encountered since I'd disembarked.

At her modest Salford terrace, she lit a fire in her back room and boiled a pan of water to make us some tea.

"I've just realised, pet," she said as she poured the hot amber liquid into her best china cups, "I don't even know your name."

"It's Jeanie," I replied shyly. "Jeanie Doyle."

"Right then, Jeanie," said Norma in her no-nonsense manner, placing a plate of biscuits on the little wooden coffee table next to me. "Let's start at the beginning."

As I sipped my tea, I poured out my life story to the woman I had met just an hour earlier. From my happy childhood back home in Ireland, to the grief of losing Mum when I was only 10, to the hell of the convent, and then finally being raped on my way home from church, I told Norma everything.

She listened without horror or disapproval, just nodded sagely and dunked her biscuits in the endless cups of PG Tips she poured from the big brown teapot. I felt as if a heavy burden had been lifted from my shoulders.

"Well, Jeanie," she said matter-of-factly, taking off her glasses and using her cotton hankie to wipe away the steam, "life has certainly thrown some blinders your way, my girl. But you're strong and I know you'll cope."

"I'm not sure that I can, Norma," I said.

Until I met her, I'd felt crushed and afraid, as if the last drops of any spirit I'd ever possessed had been sucked out of me.

"You've had some tough times, Jeanie, but you've always come through them, haven't you? Never underestimate yourself, love. You're a survivor, and I should know.

"For the last 35 years, and through no choice or fault of my own, I've been a single mum, too."

Norma recalled how, when their daughter was six months old, her husband had left her suddenly for another woman.

"It came completely out of the blue," she explained. "One morning he was there, but that evening he never came home. He was gone, just like that."

"So he didn't even talk to you or explain?" I asked. "And what about your baby? She was so young. How could he have left you both like that?"

"Because he was a wrong'un, Jeanie," she replied. "I found out afterwards that he'd gone off with this blonde piece, a barmaid ten years younger than him from down the pub. Stupid old fool, she left him eventually of course.

"I would have forgiven him," she continued, "in the beginning. If he'd realised his mistake and come back to us. But no, I waited and waited, and he didn't so much as even ask to see our beautiful baby daughter. In all those years when Sarah was growing up, he never even sent her a birthday or Christmas card. And that's what I couldn't forgive him for."

Memories of that harrowing time had clearly stirred up long-buried feelings and I could see Norma struggling to contain her pain and anger. Eventually, she cleared her throat and said calmly,

"Jeanie, if I've learnt anything from that dreadful experience, it's this: the world is full of selfish, cold-hearted people with no morals, but there are kind, caring, good folk out there too, and those are the ones we should surround ourselves with.

"Don't get me wrong, it was hard bringing up my Sarah alone. But the moment I decided I could do it, my life became a whole lot easier. You can do it, too, Jeanie. You just have to believe in yourself and get on with it, one day at a time. And if you can get through each day determined to do the right thing, you won't go far wrong."

Listening to Norma's inspirational story, I was suddenly filled with hope. This homely-looking woman who blended into the background, sweeping the church floor in her headscarf and old brown coat, was extraordinary. Despite the heartache she had suffered before her child had even celebrated her first birthday, she hadn't allowed bitterness to warp her outlook on the world. Generous, resourceful and giving, she was a shining soul who exuded goodness.

Norma took care of me like the mother I no longer had. She helped me through the final stages of my pregnancy, was by my side when I gave birth to my baby girl – who I named Sarah in honour of Norma's daughter – and showed me how to look after her.

It was also Norma who persuaded me to reveal my secret to Dad.

"He needs to know, pet," she said. "He's a grandad now but he doesn't even know it. I'm sure he'll want to see baby Sarah.

"Yes, he'll be angry at first, but that will fade in time and he'll come around. You're his only daughter and he loves you. A parent's love is pretty unbreakable, you'll see."

As I stood shivering in the freezing phone box at the end of my road, I knew I was about to test that love to its limit. In his last letter, Dad had told me that he'd just had a telephone installed, a big innovation in our little terraced house. Our first conversation over that line was about to send shockwaves through our family.

Holding the receiver in one hand, I fed a pile of sixpences into the slot with the other, my heart pounding as I plucked up the courage to break the news. When I heard his voice I launched straight in before I had time to change my mind.

"Dad, you're a grandfather," I blurted out over the crackling line. "I have a baby girl. Her name is Sarah and she's six months old."

There was a stunned silence at the other end.

"She has Mum's lips," I garbled, quickly adding, "and your eyes."

"Well this is a strange surprise, Jeanie," he said stiffly. "When did this all happen? You didn't even tell us you got married."

"I didn't get married, Dad," I whispered.

A stilted silence fell between us as I struggled to find the right words and he tried to do the maths. It didn't take him long to calculate that I would have already been pregnant when I left Dublin.

"Who's the father?" he demanded, his voice rising in fury down the phone. "Is he with you now?"

I trembled at the force of his fury.

"No, he didn't want her, Dad," I stammered. "Or me."

"But how… you didn't even have a boyfriend, did you?" he asked. I could feel his shock and confusion. "Who is this fella? He's not from our town? If I ever find out who did this to you, I'll…"

"Stop right there, Dad," I said. "It's best that you don't know who he is. And he must never find out about Sarah. It was a mistake, but I love my baby and I hope you'll love her, too."

Softening his tone, he continued, "If only you'd been honest with me, Jeanie. Why didn't you tell me? We could have worked something out."

"Such as what?" I replied, knowing and dreading what was coming next.

"Well, you could have had the baby at the convent," he said, as if explaining something to a child. "Then we would have organised for her to be adopted by a nice married couple who'd have taken care of her."

"I'm taking care of her," I interjected.

"The baby could have grown up as part of a proper family," he continued, "not with the shame of being a bastard hanging over her."

His tactless words fell on me like blows.

"She *does* have a proper family," I snapped. "You and me and my brothers. And my child will never *ever* be a bastard!"

That hideous word and Dad's mention of the convent made my blood boil. Years of resentment erupted out of me.

"As for that hell-hole you put me in for six years," I raged, "I'd never let Sarah anywhere near those evil witches. Sending me there was the worst thing you could ever have done. You hear Father Joseph talk about the devil every Sunday in church. Well that's where he lives!"

There was a sharp intake of breath at the end of the line as Dad, unaware of the years of abuse at the convent, tried to fathom what I could possibly mean.

"That's sacrilege!" he yelled. "It's not the good Sisters who disgraced themselves and brought shame on your family."

Within a matter of minutes, the chasm between Dad and me had widened even further. Would we ever be able to heal the hurt now? I didn't want to leave it like this.

"I'm sorry, Dad," I said, as the sound of frantic pips heralded the end of the most difficult phone call I had ever made. "If you ever want to see me or your granddaughter, you know where."

Before I could finish my sentence, time ran out and the call was abruptly terminated, but it felt as if my relationship with Dad had ended, too.

Although I sent him photos of baby Sarah, it would be a long time before Dad could bring himself to forgive me.

In the meantime, another man was about to arrive unexpectedly in our lives, a man who would have a profound and positive effect on me and Sarah.

Bill

When I met Bill, I was a single mum, living with my two-year-old daughter in a box room in a Salford back street.

In an extraordinary way, it was Norma – together with a batch of delicious pasties – who played cupid.

Whenever I passed the local bakery on my walks with Sarah, the mouth-watering smell of freshly baked bread would waft into the street and entice us inside. We'd always emerge with a loaf and bag of Eccles cakes, and take them home for tea.

One day an advert for part-time staff appeared in the window.

"Go for it, love," encouraged Norma. "It'll get you out of the house for a bit, earn you a few quid."

"But what about Sarah?" I asked. "I can't take her with me."

Dispelling my concerns with a wave of her hand, Norma already had the solution.

"I'll look after her, love," she said breezily. "Now you go in there and get that job."

I'd been working there for six months when in walked Bill.

A builder on a new housing development, he started coming in every lunch time for a pasty and a can of fizzy pop.

His smile and cheeky banter lit up the shop and I came to count down the hours until he made his entrance. There was something about him that made me feel alive.

He was good-looking, too. Tall with an athletic build, twinkly velvet brown eyes and an aura of pure charm, his regular visits to the shop made my day.

Truth be told, I'd never met a man like him before. He was a black fella – we called it coloured back then – and had probably experienced as much prejudice, if not more, than I had. Already we had something in common.

But there was no way in a million years I thought he'd be interested in frumpy old *me*. I'd piled on the pounds after Sarah was born and my confidence was rock bottom.

Surely it was my auburn-haired workmate Coleen, who liked to show off her big bust and long legs in tight tops and short skirts, who he was keen on?

"I'll serve him," she'd insist imperiously, pushing her way past me to the counter whenever he came into the shop, even if she was in the middle of serving someone else.

I didn't have the courage or the nerve to take on Coleen.

All the sparkiness I used to possess had been sapped out of me over the years. Although Norma, the woman I regarded as a guardian angel in human form, had saved me from the streets and offered me warmth, care and a safe haven, my self-esteem as a woman was non-existent.

When I looked in the mirror, I hardly recognised myself. The feisty young girl with bright eyes and a cheeky turn of phrase seemed like a distant memory.

"Coleen's the one he fancies anyway," I thought. Why would he want someone pale, mousy and fat when there was flame-haired Colleen, with her rouged lips and hourglass figure?

"Just give it up, Jeanie," I chided when I caught sight of my reflection in the shop window one day. "You're nothing special."

You're nothing special. It wasn't the first time those three little words had been cruelly aimed at me. And now I knew it to be true.

Suddenly the door burst open, chiming in another customer. When I looked up I saw Bill breezing swiftly towards me.

"Three meat pasties and two chicken pies, please Jeanie," he said, leaning on the counter as I nervously dealt with his order. "They're not all for me, mind," he laughed. "Some are for the boys down at the building site."

At that moment, Coleen appeared from the back of the shop.

With her hands on her hips, she positioned herself stoutly between us, and without even looking at me, said, "I'll take over from here, Jeanie."

Turning to Bill, she added with a suggestive smirk, "She's not very good with figures, see."

As she deliberately jutted out her chest, her meaning was as obvious as the conical bra beneath her tight pink sweater.

I was mortified, my face burning hot with shame.

"Is that right?" Bill shot back. "Well, I think Jeanie's good at everything."

I blinked in speechless disbelief. Was he mocking me?

Gawping like a goldfish, Coleen looked pretty dumbstruck, too.

I was flustered as I bagged up Bill's pies, thrusting his change into his hand without making eye contact. Then, as he turned to leave, he paused and swivelled around.

"Just a minute…" he began.

My heart was pounding. For a second I was afraid he was going to tell me I'd short-changed him, proving Coleen's mean mockery of my maths to be correct.

"Do you fancy going out for a drink later?" he asked.

I was so taken aback that I looked to Coleen for an answer he must have been talking to her.

"I meant with you, Jeanie," he said.

It was the first time a man had ever invited me out on a proper date.

"Yes, that would be…" I stammered.

Before I even had the chance to say "lovely", Bill was dashing out through the door, saying, "Great, I'll meet you at the pub across the road after work!"

It was as simple as that.

Coleen was bristling beside me.

"I wouldn't be able to take a darkie home to my mum and dad anyway," she sniffed. "But I suppose it doesn't matter with you, does it? You're already a bit of a black sheep. Just wait until he finds out you've got a bastard kid, you won't see him for dust."

She stalked off across the shop floor, her stilettoes stabbing the lino.

Not even Coleen's poisonous comments could rain on my parade. Now that I knew Bill had noticed frumpy old *me*, I was immune to her insults and for the rest of the day I couldn't stop smiling.

After the cold-blooded way in which Sarah had been conceived, I had given men a very wide berth. Yet somehow I sensed that Bill was different to the brute back in Ireland who had stolen my virginity.

As I got ready to meet Bill after work, I excitedly told Norma about him.

"He seems so kind," I said, brushing my chestnut hair over my shoulders, "He's tall and handsome, too."

Norma smiled at my giddy happiness as I gave her a twirl in my chosen outfit, a yellow shift dress. "Will I do?"

"You're gorgeous, pet," said Norma. "You go and enjoy yourself, God knows you deserve it.

Before I left, she couldn't resist giving me a motherly caution, "Just remember, these good-looking ones are charmers – and some are heart-breakers, too. So don't you go falling for him too soon."

I didn't think Norma had any cause for alarm. After my horrendous experience back home, I had always been on my guard around men and was scrupulously careful never to be alone with them. But when I arrived at the local pub for our date and saw Bill sitting at a corner table, my stomach turned over – he was so handsome. Perhaps I needed to be careful after all.

But I needn't have worried. Bill was not only a perfect gent, he was genuine, too, not just a good-time guy. As we talked, I discovered that he had been a bit of a Romeo in his time, but now he was looking for a more meaningful, long-term relationship.

Unlike many men I'd met before, Bill showed a real interest in me and my life, instead of making the conversation revolve around himself. And there was one big part of my life that I needed to share with him.

But was Coleen right, would he reject me for being a single mum?

"I have a little girl," I told him casually, sipping my Cinzano and lemonade while glancing quickly at his face for a reaction. "She's two years old."

"Oh, so you're divorced?" he asked.

I took a bigger gulp of my drink.

"No," I said, lowering my eyes. "It's a complicated story. But I never got married, you see."

There was a stony silence.

That's it, you've blown it now, Jeanie, I thought, too afraid to look at him and see the expression of disgust that I was sure must have transformed Bill's smiley face.

But I was wrong.

"Sorry, I didn't mean to pry," he said gently. "Tell me about it another time, if you like, Jeanie." His eyes twinkled. "At least, I hope there'll be another time, unless I've bored you rigid."

"Well, I've managed to stay awake," I smiled back. "So that's a good sign."

I wanted to jump for joy – he didn't mind about my past.

It was when I met Bill's mum that I found out why he was so accepting of me. Ivy had sailed on the Windrush all the way from Jamaica in 1948 to make a new life in England with her husband Joe. And when Joe died, she had brought up their three sons singlehandedly.

A no-nonsense nurse, Ivy didn't suffer fools gladly: she had a heart of steel but with a centre of pure gold.

It took her a while to open up and trust me, but once she did, she completely took me under her wing.

"You're one of the family now, Jeanie," she told me one evening as we sat drinking in her immaculate front parlour. "I always hoped that Bill would settle down with a nice, sensible girl like you. I never had a daughter of me own, but that's how I think of you now."

Bill was the apple of his mother's eye and even though we'd been going steady for a year, I had never really known for sure whether she thought I was a keeper for her boy, whether she thought I was good enough.

But Ivy didn't judge or even ask me about my personal history. Quiet and self-contained, she listened and observed as I courted her son Bill. And now, after a year, she had finally given me her blessing, or her royal seal of approval, as Bill and I would joke.

With my own family being so far away, I needed that anchor of love.

"That means the world to me, Ivy," I replied, rushing over to give her a hug.

Shows of affection seemed to embarrass Ivy. Even so, I could see from the soft glow in her brown eyes that she was moved.

"It's getting late," she said briskly, busying herself in the kitchen. "And the tea won't make itself!"

After the hard life Ivy had endured, I understood why she preferred to keep her emotions in check. Ten years after settling down in Salford, her beloved husband Joe had died of lung cancer, leaving her to bring up their three young sons on her own.

As well as working long hours as a nurse, she did cleaning jobs to make ends meet. For a widow with no family around her and surrounded by prejudice in a cold land, it was a tough life.

"I did what any good mother would do," she said, describing what had happened after she'd left the warm shores of Jamaica and moved to England. "There was no time to feel sorry for meself. No point fussing over spilt milk."

No wonder Bill and his two brothers were devoted to her.

"I'll see what Mum thinks," Bill would often say when it came to making a difficult decision.

But he was by no means a mummy's boy or under her thumb.

I've heard that you should observe how a man treats his mother to gauge how he will treat you, and from my experience with Bill, that was spot-on. He was a joy in the lives of both Ivy and me.

One Sunday afternoon in his mum's front parlour, he suddenly went down on one knee and asked me to marry him.

I said yes in a heartbeat as he presented me with a box containing the little sapphire engagement ring he'd bought with a month's wages.

"To match your eyes," he smiled.

"It's perfect, Bill," I breathed, as he slid it on my finger.

There was nobody I was more desperate to tell about my engagement than my Dad. The following day, when I was still buzzing with excitement, I picked up the phone to break the news to him.

"I'm getting married, Dad," I told him as soon as he picked up, "His name's Bill, and he's the loveliest–"

"You're what?"

His abrupt tone startled me. "I'm getting married, Dad! I can't wait for you to meet him, I know the both of you will get on."

I hesitated, waiting for Dad's response. But none came. "Dad?"

There was silence at the other end of the line. Then Dad slammed the phone down.

I was devastated. After all I'd been through, I wanted above all else to reconcile with my Dad and for him to be able to walk me down the aisle on my wedding day. But it wasn't to be.

"Sod them all, Bill!" I said, refusing to succumb to the dark cloud hovering over us. "I don't care what Dad thinks. We love each other and we're happy. That's all that matters."

On our wedding day, I took out the photograph of Mum as a bride and gazed at the exquisite white gown she had so lovingly kept safe for me.

"It will be for Sarah, now, Mum," I whispered, before stepping into the simple cream midi dress I had made especially for our low-key register office ceremony.

The sun shone down on us, its rays casting a golden glow through the window, as Bill and I made our vows. With Ivy and Norma as witnesses, Bill's brothers as his best men and little Sarah as our flower girl, it was a perfect day.

But I still wished Dad had found it in his heart to come, too. Deeply entrenched in his belief that he was right, he never even sent a card with his best wishes.

My daughter, thankfully, had never met her natural father, ironically a man my dad held in high esteem. The kindest, most selfless thing Bill ever did for me was to treat Sarah as if she were his own. She adored him, too. He was like a proper dad to her, not only protective and caring but also playful and fun.

He'd squeeze his tall frame into tiny spaces during her favourite game of hide-and-seek, always making sure that

Sarah won. She loved to sit on a stool in the kitchen and watch in fascination as he whipped up his delicious meals for us all, and would hold his hand until she fell asleep while he read her bedtime stories.

One day, during a rigorous bout of trampolining on her old bed, the leg broke off and we had to prop it up with books.

"I'm going to build Sarah a new bed," declared Bill. "It'll be fit for a princess."

It was, too. He carved a headboard, painted it pink and stencilled an S in the middle.

"Hey presto," he said triumphantly, proudly showing me his handiwork in his paint-spattered overalls. "What do you reckon?"

"Wow, it's beautiful," I gasped. "Sarah will *love* it."

Bill grinned from ear to ear.

"Where did you learn to make stuff like this?" I asked, in genuine awe.

A flicker of sadness crossed his face.

"Oh, I used to watch Dad when I was a kid," he replied as he quietly packed away his tools. "He was a carpenter."

Bill had indeed been taught well by the two strong role models in his life. As a young lad, he learned invaluable life skills, including how to iron, wash, clean, sew, and prepare delicious Caribbean meals from his mum's own recipes.

Preparing dishes that had been passed down through generations, Ivy was certainly the perfectionist queen of her kitchen.

"Needs more spice," she'd invariably tell Bill, dipping a spoon into the pan to sample his marinade for jerk chicken. Shaking his head with a smile, he'd pour in some more ginger and thyme, then invite her majesty to taste it again.

"Mmmm, that will do, I suppose," she'd say, secretly delighted by his redoubled effort. "Almost as good as mine."

It was a little game they'd play and the key was always to let Ivy believe that she'd won.

"I owe everything to that woman," Bill would say. "She showed me how to respect and look after myself, and to survive."

It was a talent he possessed, too.

"There's no such thing as girls' and boys' jobs," he'd tell our children. "We learn them all equally in this house."

Not only did he pass his skills on to our three kids, but also to the youngsters who joined our family during our two decades as foster parents.

A grounding, calming influence, he was a strong presence for those vulnerable children who came into our care. For many of the young girls who'd had appalling experiences with their fathers or stepfathers, and no male relatives they could look up to, suddenly here was a man they were not afraid of, who made them feel comfortable and safe.

Bill was a positive male role model to the boys we fostered, too.

He showed how a man can be sensitive and respectful without compromising his strength or masculinity.

However, he wasn't afraid to use his muscle if someone needed protecting. One evening, he jumped over a fence to catch one young thug who was harassing a girl we were fostering.

"If you ever bother her again," he warned, pinning him against a wall, "you'll have me to deal with. So if you know what's good for you, mate, you'll stop hassling her."

Bill would never have been able to get away with taking physical action like that now, of course. But back then his method worked, and that particular young man, who had subjected our girl to so much distress, never troubled her again.

Fostering A Dream

One year before young Holly was brought into our lives, Bill and I were at a party for one of Bill's workmates. At this point we already had three children – Sarah, Sophie and Stevie – and no inkling that we would soon be opening our doors to many more.

Just as we were about to leave, a friend of the host turned up late, looking frazzled.

"Does anyone happen to have a spare single bed they don't need any more?" she asked the gathering. "It's quite urgent."

"Is it for you?" I said, intrigued by her unusual request.

"No, it's for a five-year-old boy who's just been taken into care," she replied, explaining that she was a social worker. "All I've been offered so far is a grubby old mattress."

As Bill and I drove home, I couldn't get that poor lad out of my head.

"Surely someone, somewhere has a bed they can spare for the little chap?" I exclaimed in disbelief. "I can't bear to think of a child like that, taken from his family in goodness knows what appalling circumstances, having to now sleep on a mattress on the floor."

Bill was as shocked by this sad state of affairs as I was.

"I don't understand it," he said. "If the social worker had put out a request for a bed for a dog, she would have been inundated with offers. But when it comes to helping people, nobody wants to get involved."

He certainly had a valid point.

As Bill parked the car outside our house, it suddenly occurred to me that we could have helped. "We've got bunkbeds in Stevie's room!" I exclaimed "We could have taken them apart and given that boy a bed. Stevie wouldn't have minded."

I couldn't get that little lad out of my head. As I put the kettle on to make a cup of tea, I had a eureka moment. Though we felt blessed to have our three wonderful children, there was plenty of room in our hearts for more. We could make a difference, even if it was just bringing the tiniest chink of hope into a young life. By the time Bill arrived back from walking the babysitter home, I had a proposition for him.

"Hear me out and tell me what you think," I told him as he walked back into the kitchen.

"Ok, I'm all ears, Jeanie, as usual," he twinkled, stirring a spoonful of sugar into his cup.

"Look, I know we're not rich and don't live in a fabulous house," I began, "but we could put a roof over a child's head, food in their belly and clothes on their back. And we have a bed that boy could have had."

Bill was silent for a few seconds, trying to process where my thoughts were leading.

"So do you think we should adopt a child?" he asked.

I shook my head.

"No, but we could give them a safe home until they are adopted," I replied. "We could foster. We both love children and some of these kids have never experienced any affection or care in their lives. We've got a lot to give."

"But what about our kids?" he pointed out. "What would they think of it?"

It was the most obvious and important question of all. How would our three children feel about a steady stream of other children coming to live with us? Would they be happy to share their parents with a stranger?

"If even one of them seems uncomfortable with the idea, we drop it there and then," I said.

Over Sunday lunch the next day, I broached the subject.

"Kids, how would you feel about us looking after children who need help?" I began as I served up roast chicken and crispy roast potatoes.

Three pairs of eyes stared blankly back at me, a flicker of alarm taking hold as they contemplated this invasion.

"What do you mean, Mum?" asked Sarah uncertainly. "What kind of help?"

"Well," I replied slowly, "some children have unhappy lives and for many reasons can't live with their parents.

We could give them a home for a bit and help make their lives a little bit better. We'd all play a part in making that happen."

Shifting her food around her plate, Sophie bit her bottom lip and mulled it over.

"How long would it be for, Mummy?"

"Well, it could be anything from one night to a week, a month, or even a year," I replied.

"Would they have to sleep in the same bedroom as Sarah and me?"

"No, there wouldn't be space next to your bunk beds, love," I reassured her. "We'd put them in the little room down the landing. If there's more than one child, a boy could sleep in Stevie's top bunk."

Making space for a newcomer was an obstacle Bill and I had to tackle quickly, and in a small house already inhabited by five people, it would require some lateral thinking. The box room we used for storage would be the perfect space for a newcomer, once we'd rid it of all the clutter. After all, it was a box room like ours where I'd first been offered sanctuary when I was pregnant with Sarah.

"Will you love these children more than us, Mummy?" Sophie suddenly asked.

"No, pet," I replied, stroking the shiny brown curls that framed her forehead. "No-one will ever take your place with Daddy and me."

Over the next few days, all three of them had more to ask about the young newcomers, and as the thought of meeting them started to sink in, the idea was becoming more favourable to them – and intriguing.

"I'd like only boys the same age as me to live with us," announced Stevie. "Sarah's got Sophie to play with, so that's fair."

"I see your point, pet," I smiled. "But it doesn't work like that. Girls will be sent to us, too. And they'll all be different ages; some of them might even be babies."

"Oh, okay," he sighed. "But please can the boys play with me first?"

Sarah and Sophie were equally enthusiastic about the prospect of a new girl joining them.

"She can have all my teddies," declared Sarah excitedly, bundling them up in a box.

"And my Sindy dolls," added Sophie.

With the kids' blessing, Bill and I set our fostering plan in motion. The first response we received when we made enquiries with the council was more positive than I'd ever anticipated.

Mixed-race families were far rarer then than they are now, and our different heritages had sometimes provoked prejudice and bigotry.

But we were pleasantly surprised to find that in fostering it was considered an advantage, not a drawback: our blended family was deemed a good fit for foster children from different racial backgrounds.

Before we could proceed any further, the authorities needed to establish that Bill and I were a suitable couple for the job, and that everyone in our family was on board. Although not nearly as meticulous as the process today, it was still quite a thorough assessment.

When Mrs Martin, the head of social services, came to our home to meet us, it felt a bit like an interrogation.

A brusque, middle-aged woman in a royal blue, pussy-bow dress, she asked a vast range of probing questions about our families, our childhoods, what brought Bill and me together as a couple, our attitudes to bringing up children, and what we considered to be our successes in life.

As we delved deeply into our pasts, Bill's sunny, solid outlook and strength of character shone through.

However, my heart sank when I was asked about having a baby as a teenager, "out of wedlock," as Mrs Martin so clumsily phrased it.

"Will that count against me?" I asked, worried that my past might scupper our chances of fostering.

But Mrs Martin's response not only surprised me, it also showed I had misjudged her.

"On the contrary," she said in her precise, clipped tone. "We find that foster parents who have encountered and overcome problems themselves are excellent at dealing with troubled youngsters.

They have the real-life experience to understand them."

Letting out a deep sigh of relief, I looked at Bill and we both grinned. Even Mrs Martin managed a warm smile, before returning to her clipboard and cool efficiency.

"Right then," she said, sipping her tea. "Many of our children are in the care of the local authority, but our objective is to ease them into calm routines and the security of a balanced family life.

"You do understand that some will be fairly disturbed after being subjected to neglect and abuse?" she continued. "Despite this, we generally aim for the children to have supervised contact with their parents. We find that maintaining family ties is in their best interests.

"It's all a lot to take in at once," she added. "So I shall leave some reading matter for you and I'll come back to discuss it with you in more detail before a final decision is made on both sides."

We took the reams of information sheets and leaflets to read later.

"By the way," she said, smoothing down her dress as she stood up to leave. "Despite the contraceptive pill, under-age girls with no access to it or proper parental guidance are still falling pregnant. So, there's a strong likelihood that you might encounter this when you foster, Jeanie."

The training to become foster carers was not as stringent in those days as it is now. Back then it was called "Choosing to Foster" – nowadays it's "Skills to Foster" – and it only took a few days. There was a lot to learn, including new terminology such as LAC, which means "looked-after child", but we enjoyed our training.

The assessment took a lot longer – around six months. During this period we were taken right back to our childhood, our upbringing, lifestyle, schooling, beliefs and parenting style. We were also asked what challenges we might have faced in life and what had got us to where we were then.

Bill and I were seen on our own, then together, then with our children, and references were taken up, as well as police checks. Finally, we went before a panel and were asked some questions. We didn't even have to leave the room for their decision, as it was a unanimous agreement to approve us.

It seems surreal that, all these years down the line, I'm now a modern-day Mrs Martin. As part of an assessment panel, my role these days is to interview prospective foster parents, and the responsibility of finding the right environment for a child rests in my hands.

The process is far more analytical and rigorous now than when Bill and I started out. In addition to the assessment panel, would-be foster parents must also undergo a DBS (Disclosure and Barring Service) check – a government safeguard that delves into your background to find out if you have a criminal record – and visits from a social worker.

My part in the process is to gauge their suitability to foster by looking into their lives and taking them back to the year dot.

I ask about their childhoods, how their parents raised them, what their issues were, how these problems impacted them as a child, and if their parents got divorced.

They have to share everything during the assessment, no matter how many disturbing memories it might conjure up.

Even if they were tearaways as a kid, it won't necessarily count against them, because it means they have empathy and might understand why a young person is doing the same things now.

If a potential foster carer was a victim of childhood sexual abuse, they would be expected to reveal it. When they do, I ask them who helped them, if they were believed, and whether they received therapy.

If you don't search into areas like that, it could come out later when an incident with a foster child triggers off a disturbing memory. That's when the foster parent may need extra help and support for themselves.

I also have to look at the relationship of any potential foster parents. It's important that I get the measure of them as a couple. Would I feel safe leaving my own children with them? I want to see what it is about them that makes them a good partnership.

There are many soul-searching questions potential foster parents have to consider. These include how they think they would get on with a child who's very different to the kind of youngster they're used to.

If they're sent well-behaved Billy blue eyes, that's fine, but we know children like that rarely come into foster care.

As well as victims of neglect, there are children who have suffered all kinds of extreme situations, including severe sexual abuse from a paedophile ring.

Some youngsters are born to a cocaine addict, or grow up with parents who are on drugs, and are lucky to be fed.

Children in the foster family probably won't have any idea about these dreadful scenarios. They think that welcoming a new child into their home will be like a sleepover with friends of their own age. So it's a huge eye-opener for them to encounter a disturbed child who often has behavioural and anger problems.

Many kids feel excited about another child coming in, but as time goes on, they could start to feel uncomfortable about sharing their parents. Families have to work through that, to make sure that there's no difference between the way they treat their children and their foster children.

I also look to see if youngsters seem comfortable around their own parents and if they feel free to ask questions, such as, "Mummy, will I be your best child?" and "Will I have to share my things?"

The way a parent responds to such challenging dilemmas is a key indicator of how they will fare as a foster carer.

Signs of unsuitability are usually easy to spot. One couple I interviewed at their home were a prime example. The man, sitting at the head of their dining table, clearly dominated his pale, pinched wife, who sat meekly in the background.

If she so much as tried to get a few words in edgeways, he would interrupt sharply. Chain-smoking throughout our meeting, he punctuated each point he made by stubbing out his cigarettes on a pile of fag butts in a glass ashtray.

"You do realise you won't be able to smoke around the children, don't you?" I pointed out gently.

"Is that so?" he replied, defiantly lighting up another.

Noticing an unlocked cabinet in the corner, filled with bottles of whiskey, vodka and gin, I added, "And alcohol must be locked away. Some children have health issues and come from homes where their parents are alcoholics."

This would-be foster carer was evidently unfamiliar with the rules – not to mention being challenged by a mere female.

With a belligerent look on his face, he glared at me and snapped, "Nobody, especially a woman, tells me what to do in my house!"

Needless to say, I didn't recommend him.

Welcoming Holly

With only a few days to go before our new arrival, Bill and I certainly had our work cut out.

Although our case worker Carol, and Janet, the social worker, told me they would be bringing a stash of essentials such as additional terry nappies, formula milk, and baby bottles, Bill and I had to clear a space for her cot in our room and make sure the house was a baby-friendly environment again.

"Found it," said Bill triumphantly, his jeans covered in dust from the loft as he brought down the box containing the dismantled cot. "Now let's see if I can remember how to put it back together."

It didn't take Bill long to finish his task.

"There we go," he said, standing back with his hands on his hips to admire his handiwork. "Holly's new bed!"

It struck me in that poignant second that this would be the first proper bed the little mite had ever had.

As we both stared at the white cot standing in the same place as it had eight years earlier when Stevie was born, it stirred some happy memories.

"Just think, more sleepless nights, piles of nappies, endless feeds," I grinned. "It's going to be great. I only hope we've got the energy!"

Bill squeezed my hand.

"I've got a surprise for you," he said, pointing to a piece of furniture draped in a sheet in the corner.

"Remember this?" he asked, ceremoniously pulling off the dusty fabric with a flourish.

My heart leapt when I saw what was underneath.

It was the comfy nursing chair I sat on to feed our babies. Looking at its faded yellow fabric, I felt a pang of nostalgia.

"I loved that chair," I said softly, running my hand over its cushioned back. "I never thought I'd be using it again."

Suddenly, my sentimental journey was broken by our lively trio bundling into the room. And, bless them, they had come bearing gifts.

"For the baby!" cried Stevie, depositing Frankie, the purple felt snake he'd made at school, through the bars of the cot. "He'll protect Holly from monsters."

Then it was Sophie's turn.

"She can cuddle Benny, too," she said, carefully placing her favourite pale blue teddy next to Stevie's lovable reptile.

Sarah's offering was equally touching: the wooden gold and blue sun, moon and star mobile that she had treasured since she was a baby.

"I remember it fluttering in the breeze above your cot," I said, my eyes welling up as I recalled those lonely days as a single teenage mum with a young baby.

Pulling my three gorgeous youngsters towards me, I held them close.

"Thank you for the thoughtful gifts, kids," I said. "Little Holly will love them."

The night before she was due to arrive, I was so nervous and excited that I hardly slept a wink.

Running a checklist through my head, I mentally ticked off the items Holly would need, to make sure we hadn't forgotten anything. Instead of counting sheep, I was counting bottles, blankets and baby clothes.

"It'll be fine, love," said Bill softly, reaching across the bed with a reassuring hug as we finally drifted off to the land of nod. "But we're going to need every wink of shut-eye we can get."

Carol and Janet were due to bring Holly to us after lunch, so after dropping the kids off at school, Bill dashed home to help me prepare for our tiny guest's arrival.

"Just the finishing touches to put in place," he said. "Then it will be perfect."

With a flourish he scooped up Sophie and Stevie's welcome presents and placed them on top of the powder-pink blanket in her cot.

Then, after rummaging through his tool kit, he drilled Sarah's gift, the cheerful gold and blue mobile, on to the ceiling, in line with where Holly would sleep.

Watching it sparkle and twirl as it was caught by a gentle breeze, I recalled how Sarah would be totally mesmerised by the sun, star and moon as they rotated hypnotically above her cot.

"It looks amazing, Bill," I said with a smile, touched by the familiar scene that he had just recreated in front of me. "Let's hope it works its magic on Holly, too."

Carol and Janet were due to bring Holly to us at 2pm.

"I feel as nervous as a child about to take an exam," I confessed as we waited for their arrival.

Although my emotions flitted from excitement to apprehension and back again, I just knew that we were doing the right thing.

Suddenly the doorbell chimed and my stomach did a somersault. I shot a glance into the hallway and saw Carol's shoulder-length dark hair and Janet's distinctive navy raincoat through the front door's misty glass. But most important of all, the dark blue hood of Holly's pram was visible, too.

I turned nervously to Bill.

"Well, this is it," I whispered. "I'm feeling a bit jittery."

Bill gave my hand a reassuring squeeze. "I'll make the tea, you answer the door."

Heart pounding, I did as he suggested.

"Hello, Jeanie," Carol beamed. "We have a little visitor for you."

"I can't wait to meet her," I smiled, ushering them inside. "Come on in out of the cold."

Carefully leveraging the pram over the front step, Carol stepped into the hallway, followed by Janet, who plonked two bags of baby paraphernalia on the floor.

While Janet methodically unpacked the baby bags, Carol detached Holly's carrycot from its carriage and manoeuvred it through the narrow doorway into our warm sitting room.

"Is she awake?" I asked softly, aware that no baby sounds were coming from inside.

"No, she's just dropped off in the car," said Carol.

Tip-toeing over to the carrycot, I leaned down and peered beneath the hood. And there she was.

Wrapped up warm in a fluffy white blanket, Holly was softly slumbering, her rosebud lips and tiny button nose twitching slightly as she dreamt, no doubt of her next feed.

With her apple cheeks and wisps of curly dark hair poking out from beneath her white woollen bonnet, she looked like a cherub.

"Welcome, baby Holly," I whispered, hit by an unexpected pang of maternal tenderness. I wanted to scoop her up and hold her tight, so that no harm could ever come to her.

"She's a beautiful baby, Carol," I said. "Like a little angel."

"It's the calm before the storm, Jeanie," she laughed. "She can be very loud when she's hungry!"

I recalled only too vividly how a baby can be as quiet as a mouse one minute, and bawling its head off the next.

"In that case, Holly will fit in well," I said. "There's usually so much noise going on in this house that she'll have competition on the volume front."

Suddenly, the clattering of china cups and plates on my hostess trolley proved my point.

"You see what I mean," I quipped, which made even Janet's characteristic sour expression break into a grin. "We're a lively lot."

On that note, the door flew open and Bill trundled in with the squeaky trolley.

"Hello, ladies!" he said brightly, placing a tray heaving with cakes, a big pot of tea and our finest bone china cups on to the pine table. Bill hadn't forgotten our new guest, either.

"I've just made up a feed for Holly," he said. "By the time she wakes up it'll be the right temperature for her."

"Thanks love," I said. "You're ahead of us all."

But Janet was harder to please. "Holly's fed on demand during the night as well as throughout the day," she said, "so don't expect too much sleep in the weeks ahead of you."

With a wry grin out of Janet's line of vision, Carol rolled her eyes.

Janet was, as my mother would say, so whippet-thin you could thread a needle with her. A dry old stick and abrasive to the point of rudeness, she seemed to want to wrong-foot you at every turn, which felt a bit like being repeatedly stung by a jellyfish.

Accustomed to the many bossy females in his life, Bill was unfazed by Janet and simply topped up her tea.

Suddenly, the bundle of white blankets in the pram started to stir and cry faintly. Holly was beginning to wake up.

Carol jumped up and gently lifted Holly out of her pram.

"Would you like to give Holly her bottle, Jeanie?" she asked as the little one's cry became more insistent.

I nodded enthusiastically.

Taking her into my arms, I rested her head in the crook of my elbow while supporting her body with my left hand. She stopped crying almost immediately and nestled into me.

I'd forgotten how it felt to hold a baby, so small, so light, so innocent and vulnerable, and most of all, so completely dependent on me.

"Hello, Holly," I whispered.

Sensing a new person around her, this exquisite baby girl made a snuffling sound and opened her eyes. They were the most beautiful colour I'd ever seen. An unusual deep violet-blue, they seemed to look straight into my soul, as if to ask, "Who are you?"

"I'm Jeanie, sweetheart," I murmured. "I'm going to be looking after you for a while."

As I touched her tiny hand, she gripped my fingers and started looking around for her feed.

"Here you go, Holly," I smiled, as Janet passed me her bottle. "Your lunch."

As she sucked hungrily on the teat, I wondered if her mother had ever shared a tender moment like this with her newborn baby.

"Still no sign of Angela?" I asked.

Carol shook her head.

"Not yet," she replied. "But we're still hopeful. There are no records of this baby being born in any of the local hospitals, so she may well have given birth on her own. In that case, she'll need medical attention."

"She must be out there somewhere," I said. "Probably closer than we think."

Blissfully oblivious to any of the complications that had blighted the beginning of her life, baby Holly continued contentedly with her feed.

By the time Carol and Janet had left, she was asleep in my arms.

"I'll put her in her cot now, Bill," I said quietly, so as not to wake her. "She'll need a nap before the kids come home from their last day of school."

Moving carefully, I carried her upstairs and placed her in her crib, tucking the pale pink blankets around her.

"Sleep tight, little one," I whispered, closing the bedroom door softly behind me.

Afraid that the slightest sound might wake her, Bill and I crept around downstairs, unpacking Holly's bottles, powdered formula milk, nappies and the few outfits she had been given by the nurses at the hospital.

"It's reminds me of old times," grinned Bill as he padded around the kitchen. "I'd almost forgotten what it was like."

Suddenly, he accidentally clanked a saucepan and a tinny echo reverberated throughout the house. We froze, straining our ears to listen out for Holly's cry.

But when I popped upstairs to look in on her, she was still sleeping peacefully.

"She is one very tranquil little baby," I smiled.

It was, however, just the calm before the storm. After Bill picked up the kids from school, the three of them bundled through the front door and, bright eyed with excitement, charged into the kitchen.

"Where is she, Mum?" Sarah asked breathlessly. "Where's baby Holly?"

"She's asleep in her cot upstairs," I whispered, mashing butter into the potatoes for tea. "Try to be quiet in case she wakes up."

But my plea went unheeded and as their footsteps thundered upstairs, I heard a tiny muffled cry. Baby Holly was awake.

"You go up and see to her," said Bill, who had just finished setting the table and was draining the carrots. "I'll sort tea."

"Thanks love," I replied, handing him my pinnie.

"By the way, Bill," I added, with a wink. "Welcome back to baby-ville!"

Upstairs I was greeted by the touching sight of our enthusiastic trio cooing over our cute new guest.

"She's like a little doll," said Sophie, resting her chin on the side of the cot.

"Can I cuddle her please, Mam?" pleaded Sarah. "I'll be very careful."

Stevie was keen to make a claim on baby Holly, too.

"Right everyone," he said matter-of-factly, opening his school bag and bringing out a book. "I'm going to read her a story. Do you think she'll like Paddington Bear?"

Ruffling his hair, I put my arm around him as our little visitor wriggled restlessly beneath her blankets.

"After tea, you can all help me get Holly ready for bed," I said. "Sarah, you're in charge of the nappies and bottles, and Sophie can choose what sleepsuit she wears tonight.

"Stevie, you can read a bedtime story from your Christmas book. Holly's spending her first ever Christmas with us so I'm sure she'd love to hear all about Santa and his reindeer."

As the kids' faces lit up, Bill called up to us from the hallway.

"Tea time, gang! Shepherd's pie followed by sponge pudding and custard."

As our three famished youngsters clambered downstairs to the kitchen, I gently lifted Holly from her cot and held her close.

"You must be hungry too, little one," I murmured as she stared at me with her violet-blue eyes.

Sitting at the dining table with Holly in my arms, I gave her another bottle while the kids tucked in to their tea.

They couldn't keep their eyes off her and cleared their plates in record time so that they could get on with the jobs I had given them earlier.

"Story time!" said Stevie triumphantly, running to fetch his treasury of Christmas tales.

"Not yet, silly, it's bath time first," protested Sarah, as she and Sophie jumped up from the table. "Come on, let's choose a sleepsuit for the baby."

The excitement of Holly joining our family took its toll on us all, but in a good way. Later, when I peered into the semi-darkness of the kids' rooms, they were sleeping like babies.

I sighed with relief and turned to Bill.

"Right, let's have a nightcap before we turn in," I said. "I fancy a hot chocolate with a tot of brandy."

As I sipped my drink, I couldn't stop thinking about Holly being abandoned on the church steps.

"She would have been so hungry she must have cried for her mother all night," I said. "Do you think she knew she was unwanted and will grow up feeling that loss?"

Bill shrugged and put it into a practical perspective.

"I don't know about any of that, Jeanie," he said. "But what I do know is that Holly is no longer abandoned or outside in the cold. She's safe here with us, tucked up in her cot in a warm house, being fed and hugged and doted on by all of us.

"Even if her mother never comes forward to claim her," he continued, "she'll be adopted by a family who'll love her. Whatever happens, she has a happy future ahead of her."

Bill was right and it was reassuring to think that, as long as there are people willing to give a child a home, to adopt or foster, there's always hope for the discarded, forsaken kids of this world.

Throughout my journey as a foster mum, I discovered that, despite the turmoil these youngsters often brought into our household, they also inspired genuine affection and even love.

What surprised me was how swiftly a baby who was not my own could pull at my maternal heartstrings.

The first few days and nights passed in a blur of nappy changing, bottle feeds, and cuddling Holly on the nursing chair next to her cot.

I had almost forgotten how demanding a baby could be, but Bill helped out as much as he could, taking turns with the night shifts while I caught up on my sleep.

We discovered early on that the only thing that would stop Holly crying was to hold her close.

Each time I stealthily made my way to the door, she sensed that I was about to leave her. Was it because her mother had left her on the steps of the church only a week or so earlier?

Making sure that I gave my trio enough attention with a baby in our midst was a balancing act. Thank goodness for Bill and his culinary skills.

While I looked after Holly, he would feed the family with his delicious dishes. Then, when I needed to eat, Nana Ivy would play her part, too. With Holly's little face peering over her shoulder, Ivy walked her up and down, rocking her to sleep with the rhythmic movement of her hips.

Nana Ivy seemed to have a magic touch with babies. She had helped to nurse Sophie and Stevie after they were born and the way she sang her Jamaican lullaby, *Hush Mama Baby*, was hypnotic enough to send us all into the land of nod.

Though Holly was angelic by day, she cried with a vengeance at night. One evening Stevie looked at her intently as she was bawling and after pondering for a moment, declared, "When her mummy gets here, I hope Holly won't cry any more."

I couldn't have agreed more, but in truth I had no idea if that day would ever come.

A First Christmas

Holly's little face was a picture when around her Sarah, Sophie and Stevie excitedly decorated the tree. After squealing about where each ornament should go, they started the annual bicker over whose turn it was to place the angel on the top.

"I think that as it's Holly's first Christmas, we should give that turn to her," I suggested, watching for their reaction.

Bill and the kids turned to look at me as if they thought I had gone mad.

"Have you been on the sherry again, Jeanie?" Bill laughed, while my outraged trio just stared at me in horror.

"Well, obviously, Holly can't do it herself," I explained, "so Daddy, who's very tall, will place it on the top of the tree for her."

My idea was a hit.

"Yes!" cheered Sophie. "This year the angel is for Holly."

I had tried to bring up my children not to be selfish, which is no easy task with three high-spirited youngsters. But sometimes they did me proud.

Scrabbling through the box of decorations, Stevie pulled out the bundle of white tissue paper containing the ornament I made when Sarah was just a babe in arms.

An angel with wings made from a white paper doily, a halo of silver tinsel and a lacy handkerchief dress she had seen better days, but to us she epitomised the magic of Christmas.

"Make a wish, Holly," said Sarah.

It is a tradition in our house that whoever puts the angel on the tree can make a wish. As Bill reached up to put her in place, I silently made one for Holly.

"I get the feeling this wish will come true for you," I whispered, holding her up in front of the multi-coloured fairylights.

"Well, let's see what the New Year brings, Jeanie," Bill said with a wink. "In the meantime, these three little angels need to go to bed and get some sleep. Otherwise they'll be too tired for Christmas!"

Playfully giving chase, he raced after them while they shrieked with laughter all the way up the stairs.

Dressed in their pyjamas and buzzing with excitement, they began their Christmas Eve ritual of leaving a mince pie and sherry for Santa.

"Hold your horses, young man," laughed Bill as our eight-year-old son reached for a bottle of Harvey's Bristol Cream in our drinks cabinet. "*I'll* pour a glass for Santa while you find some carrots for Rudolph."

With a pile of presents to wrap and stockings to fill, we needed our boisterous youngsters to calm down and get some sleep.

Tilting my head towards the door, I gave Bill our subtle sign for bedtime.

"Right, kids," he said. "Santa won't come if he knows you're still awake. Last one upstairs is a rotten egg!"

After giving Holly her bottle, I quietly carried her up to her cot and tucked her in snugly. I watched her for a while as she lay sleeping, warm and safe. She might not have her mother, but she had us.

Tired after a long day, all I wanted to do was collapse into bed and sleep until morning, but there were still more presents to wrap and stockings to fill before I could even consider it. Just as I had done for each of my three babies, I had made Holly a red felt Christmas stocking embroidered with her initial.

Finally, as the clock struck midnight, Bill and I munched and swigged Santa's gifts before heading, exhausted, to bed.

It seemed strange to be woken up at 4am on Christmas morning, not by the sound of the kids ripping open the presents in their stockings, but by Holly crying for her first feed of the day.

I rolled over to the side of the bed and, bleary-eyed, pulled on my dressing gown and padded over to her cot.

"Happy Christmas, little one," I whispered, carefully lifting her out. "Let's take you downstairs for your breakfast."

Her cry of hunger was becoming more insistent, so I quickly made up her formula milk. "How much simpler would it be," I thought, "if her mother was here to breastfeed?"

Sitting back against the soft sofa, I gave Holly her bottle. While she guzzled away, I glimpsed through the window the young robin that lived in our garden, his red breast contrasting vividly with the sparkly white frost as he bobbed around relentlessly, looking for food.

The ground was too hard and frozen for him to find insects or worms, but the famished bird finally found the breadcrumbs I'd sprinkled and was pecking away to his heart's content.

It occurred to me then that sometimes nature needs a helping hand for survival, a nurturing stop-gap before the ground thaws and a baby's mother returns to claim and feed her child.

"Where are you, Angela?" I murmured into the silence. "Your baby needs you."

Was she safe and well, or suffering in silence and unable to tell?

Wherever she was at that moment, I instinctively knew that she would not be able to stop thinking about her baby girl. In desperation she had wrapped her in her own coat and placed her on the steps of a church; surely she was praying that her baby was safe and warm and loved?

Looking at Holly, so innocent, vulnerable and trusting, as she gazed up at me with her violet-blue eyes, I wanted to cry.

This was the first Christmas Day of her life, yet here she was with me, a stranger, when she should have been with her mother.

Suddenly, the early morning silence was broken by the sound of footsteps thundering overhead. Sophie and Stevie raced breathlessly down the stairs with Sarah and Bill trailing close behind.

"Has he been, has Santa been?" cried Stevie.

"Yes, he has!" squealed Sophie, seeing the empty mince pie plate on the kitchen table. "He drank all his sherry, too. And his reindeer ate their carrots. Yippee!"

Swiftly bringing up the rear was Sarah, who despite telling me in private that she was far too old to believe in Father Christmas, was as eager as they were to reach her stocking.

Behind her, Bill lumbered into the kitchen in his dark blue dressing gown.

"Merry Christmas, love!" he said with a wink as Sarah, Sophie and Stevie gleefully tore open the presents we had so carefully wrapped the day before.

"Time for a brew..." he grinned and put the kettle on, as whoops and cheers resounded throughout the house.

With Holly in my arms, I watched the pure joy of the Christmas present chaos.

"Just a minute, you lot," I said after a while. "Aren't we forgetting someone?"

The three of them looked up quizzically from their Christmas booty.

"Oh, yes, of course," said Sarah. "It's Holly's turn!"

Charging over to Holly's stocking, Stevie pulled out the first package and shook it next to his ear.

"It's a rattle!" he declared, waving it exuberantly while running around in circles.

Sophie unwrapped the next package, a blanket I had secretly crocheted for her in a shade of violet to match her eyes.

"I didn't know Father Christmas could knit!" declared Stevie indignantly.

"He can't, silly," said Sophie, placing her hands on her hips and rolling her eyes. "He has elves to do this. Everyone knows that, Stevie!"

Stifling a giggle, Sarah reached for the final present and unwrapped it in front of Holly at the table.

"Look, it's a book of nursery rhymes," she said, sweetly stroking Holly's forehead. "I'll read all of them to you later."

The Christmas excitement was all too much for our little visitor. As her eyelids began to droop, I took her upstairs to her cot and settled her down to sleep.

Not even the squeaky floorboard on the landing seemed to disturb her, which I took as a sign that a sense of security and calm had descended on the little mite.

Downstairs, while the kids played with their toys in the front room, Bill and I retreated to the kitchen to get cracking on our festive Christmas dinner.

We made a great team, Bill and I, and at Christmas in particular we were a well-oiled machine with a routine that worked like clockwork.

"Glass of sherry, love?" he asked, switching on the oven and seasoning the turkey with a liberal splash of fresh lemon and lime juice, salt and pepper, spicy herbs and strips of bacon.

"Make it a bucket!" I grinned.

Later, with lunch bubbling, boiling and roasting away, Nana Ivy announced her arrival with the usual three rings of the doorbell. She was looking as immaculate as ever in her smart olive green suit with a matching hat and the white gloves she always wore to church.

"Merry Christmas, Jeanie!" she beamed as I welcomed her in with a hug. "Now where's that boy Bill and me gorgeous grandchildren?"

As she bustled into the sitting room, the kids charged screeching towards her.

"Hands up who would like a present?" she said as the trio gathered eagerly around Ivy and her seemingly bottomless Mary Poppins style leather handbag.

As quick as a flash, they put their hands straight up into the air, and Ivy rewarded them with three parcels containing the most exquisite hand-knitted Christmas jumpers.

"So where's the little one, Jeanie?" she asked. "I've made baby Holly a special present."

It was almost as if she sensed that her name had been mentioned, because the next thing we knew, there was a muffled cry from upstairs.

"That child has a healthy pair of lungs on her, Jeanie," said Ivy with a smile. "Mark my words, she's a strong girl, that one. I think it's time for Nana Ivy to give her a cuddle.

"Oh, and Bill," she called, playfully placing her first order of the day while her son prepared Christmas dinner in the kitchen. "Where's me brandy and Babycham? Mum's getting very thirsty in here."

When I brought Holly down from her cot, her face all sleepy yet alert, Ivy put down her glass and reached out to hold her.

"Come to Nana," she said, gently taking her in her arms. "I have a present for you sweetie."

Sarah did the honours, unwrapping a pair of the finest white booties and a matching bonnet with a dark green holly pattern knitted into them.

"For your first Christmas, dear Holly," said Ivy, proudly undoing the silky white ankle ribbons and slipping the booties she had made on to her tiny feet. Soothed by the softness of the wool, Holly wriggled and pointed her toes.

Later, full of turkey, Christmas pudding and Asti Spumante, Bill, Ivy and I slumped on the sofa in our paper crowns, while the kids played with their Christmas toys.

"Time for the Queen's speech," smiled Bill. "And no Mum, I don't mean you."

Ivy swiped him with the end of a cracker and then sat up, smart and alert. "Pay attention, son. Respect for Her Majesty, please."

As the monarch spoke of the importance of unity and togetherness, my thoughts turned to Holly's desperate young mum.

Wicked Girl

"Where is she now?" I wondered, imagining how anxious and afraid she must be feeling about the fate of this little bundle, her baby, nestled snugly in *my* arms.

Angela

Every New Year fills me with hope and a sense of fresh new beginnings. This year, with baby Holly in our midst, growing bigger, stronger and more alert by the day, I felt sure we would receive news of her mother soon.

Sure enough, as I was taking down our Christmas decorations on twelfth night, the telephone rang.

"Jeanie, it's Carol. I've got some news," she said, sounding cautiously upbeat.

"Is it about Holly's mum?"

"Yes, we've found her.

"Does she want to see her baby?"

There was a pause.

"Well, yes," she hesitated. "She's keen to make sure her daughter is healthy and well. But there are complications and some sensitive information. Can I talk to you about this face to face?"

Within ten minutes of our call, Carol was ringing the doorbell.

"Come in," I whispered as I opened the front door, pointing to the ceiling to indicate that Holly was asleep upstairs. "Let's go into the sitting room."

No sooner had Carol sat down than she took a deep breath and proceeded to fill me in.

"As we guessed from the name tag in the anorak that Holly was wrapped in, Angela is her mum," she explained. "She's a very young girl, too; she'd only just turned 15 when she gave birth to her."

I shook my head at what Angela must have gone through on her own.

"Just before Christmas, she collapsed at school," continued Carol. "She was bleeding and had a fever. When doctors examined her, they discovered that she'd recently had a baby and was suffering from an infection. She's fortunate that they caught the infection in time. She's lucky to be here."

"How about Holly's father, did she tell anyone his name?"

"Well, at first Angela was too ill to talk about him," Carol explained. "When the hospital tried to contact her parents, only her father – who works shifts at a factory – turned up, and she seemed pretty terrified of him.

"Everyone assumed it was because she was feeling ashamed. He was quite a forceful man, shouting at his daughter and the staff, saying that they had no right to question her and he was going to take her home. But she was too ill, of course, and they wouldn't let him."

The vision of an angry father brought back a painful memory of my own dad and how furious he had been when he found out I was a single teenage mum.

"Poor kid," I murmured. "As if she didn't have enough on her plate without her dad kicking off."

"Well, it gets worse, Jeanie," Carol sighed. "He started yelling at Angela, calling her every name under the sun, like slut and tart, claiming that she was out of control with lads all over the place."

"So why didn't he go and hold these fellas to account?" I asked. "Why should she bear the brunt of the blame while some Tom, Dick or Harry walked away scot-free?"

"But that's just it, Jeanie," explained Carol. "There were no boys. She'd never even had a boyfriend."

Now I understood.

"So she was raped," I said.

"Yes, I'm afraid so, Jeanie."

Finally, an exhausted and terrified Angela had confided in one of the nurses and told her that the rapist who made her pregnant was her father.

"He had tried to make it seem like she was promiscuous," explained Carol. "He couldn't be sure that she hadn't told the hospital staff what had really happened, you see, so he was covering his tracks."

The shock hit me with such force that I suddenly felt nauseous.

"He what?" I gasped. "I hope he's locked up."

"Well, the police took him in for questioning, but we don't know if they kept him in or if he's been released. For now, we're focusing on Angela and her baby."

"So where's Angela's mum in all this?" I asked.

But there was even more to this sordid tangled web than I had ever imagined.

"Her mother knows nothing about it yet," said Carol. and she went to recount the horrific story that Angela had confided to the young nurse.

After her mum went off with another man, her dad started drinking heavily, knocking back neat whisky from first thing in the morning to last thing at night when he'd collapse in a stupor.

I could imagine the fear and neglect Angela would have suffered.

"One evening he came home and took out his frustrations on Angela," she continued. "She looks a lot like her mother Kathleen, which he hated – and apparently during the attack he kept calling her by her mother's name."

According to Angela's teachers, he had been a good father to her until then. But I knew from experience some men can present a respectable façade to the world, yet turn into monsters behind closed doors.

"The brute raped her, his own daughter," I sighed. "What sort of father does that?"

Carol shook her head.

"I don't understand it either, Jeanie," she said. "We just have to make sure Angela and Holly are safe, and leave the police to deal with her dad."

Throughout my career as a foster carer, I have been obliged to remain civil when I meet child abusers, whatever my personal feelings. As a foster carer, you are obliged to maintain a professional stance of objectivity: you aren't allowed to judge or rebuke them, or make assumptions about their character.

Maintaining this code of conduct has been a struggle for me in cases like Angela's, where sexual abuse and violence are involved.

Despite what a parent has done to damage their child, contact between them is encouraged. No matter how hard I found this, especially if the parent turned up drunk or just didn't turn up at all, I always had to keep in mind that this was their family, warts and all, and children would generally prefer to be with their kin than a stranger.

A bad family was often better than no family at all, it seemed.

In Angela's case, however, it was unlikely that she would ever again want to see the man who had raped her.

"When she found out she was pregnant, I expect she was in denial for a bit?"

Carol nodded knowingly.

"I realised that you of all people would understand," she said gently. As my case worker, Carol knew all about my past.

The scar was still there deep inside, and even after all these years, it would never quite heal completely.

"You feel so ashamed, guilty, and scared," I recalled. "One minute you're in denial, the next you're in a panic. But the over-riding memory I have of that bleak time is of feeling totally alone."

"That's exactly what it was like for Angela too," said Carol. "She just tried to carry on as normal and when her bump started to show, she hid it under baggy clothes.

"She even managed to conceal it from her teachers and friends at school. Her sports mistress was the only person who became suspicious after Angela started faking notes from her parents to excuse her from PE. But when she asked Angela what was wrong, she claimed to be suffering everything from flu to a twisted ankle and heavy periods."

It didn't come as any surprise to me to hear that a young girl can keep her pregnancy a secret until she reaches her due date: after all, I had done the same when I was expecting Sarah. And it seems that what your family and friends do not expect to see, remains invisible.

"What about the birth?" I asked.

Childbirth is daunting enough in hospital, when you are surrounded by doctors and nurses, and all the equipment and pain relief you need. But to go into labour on your own, with none of those medical experts on hand to help, must have been terrifying.

"Her waters broke one morning while she was getting ready for school," said Carol. "She didn't really know what was happening, so after her dad left the house to go to work, she got into the bath to clean herself up and that's when she went into labour."

"At least the warm water must have helped ease the pain of the contractions," I said, remembering how I'd got Bill to run me a bath when mine started with Sophie and Stevie. "Was she in labour for long?"

"She thinks it was a few hours, and without any pain relief she says it was agony. She's lucky to be alive after going through all that on her own."

I put my hand over my face and groaned.

"Mary and Jesus, she must have been crying out," I said. "Didn't any of the neighbours hear? When I gave birth you would have heard me in the next town!"

"None of the neighbours the police spoke to heard anything apparently," Carol shrugged. "It's incredible, isn't it, considering how thin the walls are in those council flats."

I realised suddenly what Angela had done.

"She must have put a towel in her mouth, bitten down on that," I said. "It's what my mother and grandmother did during childbirth back in Ireland."

Carol went on to explain that, after placing Holly on her chest, she lay back in the bath exhausted. Then, eventually, she reached over the bath for a pair of nail scissors and used them to cut the umbilical cord.

It was not a clean cut that was evident to the nurses when they looked at Holly. Then, instead of the feed and cuddle that most newborns get, a shocked Angela just desperately wanted to get rid of the evidence that anything had happened. After draining away the blood-filled bathwater, she had wrapped Holly in a towel and hidden her in the basket she used for cookery lessons at school.

Later, while her father was still boozing down the pub, she crept out and left the basket on the steps of the church.

"Angela used to go there with her family a long time ago," said Carol. "So she knew Father Gerry and asked to see him when she was recovering in hospital. She felt so guilty for abandoning Holly and was terrified that she might not have survived the night.

"Their meeting turned into a bit of a confessional, really," she continued. "Father Gerry was great, thankfully. He didn't lecture or judge. Just listened."

With a tentative smile, Carol got to the purpose of her visit.

"This brings me to another caring person I know," she said softly. "You, Jeanie.

"Although Angela is still traumatised after her ordeal, she would like to see her baby again. She's not sure yet if she will ever feel able to be a proper mother to her, but she'd like to find out if it's at all possible. I can't think of a better person to smooth the path to that reunion than you."

Still reeling from the traumatic story I'd just heard, I understood now what was being asked. Angela would join Holly in our home and my role would be to show her how to look after her baby.

"It would be a short-term arrangement," Carol assured me, "until we can organise a more permanent plan for them both. Together, or apart."

Although Angela was still just a child herself, there was no hard-and-fast rule about whether underage girls would keep their babies or give them up for adoption. When social services became involved, we tended to work through the situation so that the young woman could reach her own decision.

In my experience, however, a girl who has been raped – especially by her own father or another member of her family – is unlikely to want to keep the child, especially if it looks like the person who attacked them.

Would Angela be willing to bring up a daughter who might turn out to be a constant reminder of that attack?

I had never seen a photograph of Angela, but whenever I pictured her, I imagined her resembling a teenage version of Holly.

The day she arrived to stay, I opened the front door and there she was. The similarity between her and Holly was startling.

She had the same wavy dark hair and violet eyes, and as she glanced at me and then looked shyly away, it felt as if it was a future Holly standing there.

With her pale skin and willowy figure, Angela had a fragile, other-worldly aura and vulnerability that immediately made me feel protective towards her.

Shivering on the doorstep, she smiled nervously and lowered her eyes.

"We've been looking forward to meeting you, Angela," I smiled, guiding her inside. "Think of this as your home too, love."

As I led her into the kitchen, I couldn't help noticing how her shoulder blades were jutting through the scanty fabric of her belted raincoat. She looked as if the slightest breeze would blow her away like a feather.

"Thank you Mrs."

"Call me Jeanie, pet," I interrupted. "Now let's get you a hot drink. And a sandwich. Here you go, I've just made a plate of them. Cheese and tomato? Salmon paste? There's cakes, too."

Angela's face lit up at the tasty spread on the table in front of her.

Encouraged by the warm welcome, she looked at me with her wide blue eyes and asked, "May I have a cheese and tomato sandwich, please? And some cake?"

I'd never encountered such impeccable manners in a girl of her age before and they were matched by her dainty demeanour.

"Do take a seat, love," I urged, gently easing her into a chair as she hovered uncertainly next to the table. "Help yourself to anything you like."

While Angela delicately nibbled a sandwich and sipped a glass of orange squash, I spoke in hushed tones to Janet, the social worker, in the hallway.

"She's such a lovely girl," I whispered. "And so gentle. But is there anything else I should know before I take her up to see Holly?"

Janet shook her head.

"We've assessed her emotional state and whether she's ready to meet her baby," she replied. "In our opinion she's calm and stable enough for this reunion. But we will have to gauge how well it goes, Jeanie, before we know what happens next."

"You mean, decide whether Angela should keep Holly?"

Janet pursed her lips and nodded.

"Yes, but what happens doesn't just depend on whether she wants to keep her," she said. "She needs to understand the full extent of what it means to be a mum with a baby. If she's not capable of looking after her day in and day out, we'll have to find another solution."

"Yes, I see what you mean," I said, remembering how it felt to be a teenage mum myself. "No more fun or freedom or time to yourself. Your needs come last. Speaking from experience, having to buckle down to the responsibility for another little person seems like the hardest job in the world."

Janet sighed wearily.

"What's more, Jeanie," she added, "Angela won't be old enough to leave school until she's 16. In the eyes of the law she's still a child herself and will have to return to school."

Weighing up the circumstances of how her baby was conceived, her age and the fact there was no mother on the scene, it seemed like the prospect of Angela being able to keep her baby was very slim indeed.

We would find out in the days, or even weeks, ahead.

While I understood the reasoning behind what could only be described as an experiment, I shuddered to think of the emotional fallout if Angela wanted to keep Holly but was incapable of looking after her properly – or if she rejected her baby completely.

Sometimes the happy endings we hope for simply don't work out, and it's in the best interests of both the baby and the mother for an adoption to take place.

However, before we reached that point of no return, I was determined to help this young girl to the best of my ability, by showing her how to look after her child.

"If Angela proves that she can and wants to do it, where will she and Holly live in the long term?" I asked Janet.

With her mother no longer on the scene, there was no way Angela would have been allowed to return to her family home to look after her baby on her own.

"We're working on that," she replied. "At the moment, we're trying to track down close relatives, such as her grandparents. Her mother would have been our first point of call, of course, but we haven't been able to trace her yet."

With no mother around and a father set for a custodial sentence, Angela's future seemed uncertain.

Yet there was one chink of light in the immediate path ahead: baby Holly. While they were both under my roof and in my care, my role was to help them bond and to teach Angela the skills of motherhood.

"I'll settle Angela in and keep you and Carol informed," I told Janet as she began to edge towards the door. "By the way, where are her things?"

The only luggage I could see was the small navy suitcase she had placed at the bottom of the stairs.

Janet nodded towards it, saying, "It's all she has to make do with at the moment. She was too upset to go back inside the house. But once we can gain access, I'll be able to bring out more of her belongings."

Looking at Angela's petite frame, I suddenly had a thought. Despite being two years older than Sarah, she was about the same size — a comparison that chilled my heart after what Angela had suffered.

"She can borrow some of Sarah's clothes until then, Janet," I said.

"Right you are, Jeanie," Carol replied in her no-nonsense manner. "Now if there are any problems at all, don't hesitate to let me know straight away."

Learner Mum

When I returned to the kitchen, I stopped in my tracks. Angela was at the kitchen sink, quietly drying her plate and glass tumbler with a tea towel.

"That's very sweet of you, love," I said, astonished at how helpful she was already, especially as my kids usually needed prompting to tackle any household chores. "I can see that you're well trained!"

"I always do the washing up at home," she said, self-consciously tucking a strand of hair behind her ear.

She paused and corrected herself.

"Well, I used to…" she added with a forlorn expression.

I smiled at her. She had arrived only half an hour earlier but it must have seemed like hours to her, considering that she was here to see the baby she had abandoned on the church steps.

"Before my three kids come home from school and cause mayhem, I think there's someone you'd like to meet, Angela," I said softly. "Are you ready, love?"

Her eyes widened nervously and she nodded.

"Yes, where is Maria?" she whispered, almost apologetically.

"Maria?"

"Her name," she said, "I named her before I took her to the church."

It had never occurred to me that Angela would have named her child before leaving her on the steps. But maybe this was a good sign: perhaps it meant that, despite the violent way in which Maria had been conceived, Angela had cared about her enough to give her a name.

"I'm so sorry, love," I said. "We didn't know, so we've been calling her Holly, you see, because it was Christmas."

"Yes, it's all right, don't worry," she said, looking flustered. "Holly's a lovely name."

"Shall we go upstairs and see if Maria's awake?" I asked gently, watching her reaction to see if she was ready. "She'll probably want her feed soon."

Angela nodded, but her eyes were anxious.

"Don't worry, pet," I said reassuringly. "We'll just see how you feel. If you don't want to hold or feed her, that's fine."

"No, I'd like to see her now," she whispered.

As I invited her to walk up the stairs in front of me, I noticed that she was trembling.

Once she had reached the top of the landing, she hesitated. Her eyes darted back and forth to each of the five doors, wondering which her baby was sleeping behind.

"It's just here, on the left," I said, but she held back from opening the door. "I didn't put the cot in your room just yet. Thought it best to give you time to settle in."

Angela looked relieved.

As I stepped forward to open the door to my bedroom, Maria started to cry.

I led the way, with Angela following slowly behind, and as I picked up the crying baby from the cot, Maria calmed down and rested her head against my shoulder.

"She's grown a lot," said Angela, looking at her with a combination of fascination and fear.

Maria tilted her head towards her, their violet-blue eyes locked in what appeared to me to be mutual recognition.

"Would you like to hold her?"

Angela nodded and cautiously reached out for the bundle in my arms. But holding her baby, who was over a month old, didn't come naturally to her, of course. Instead of letting Maria nestle close to her chest, she carried her awkwardly, keeping a distance between them.

Yet Maria stopped crying immediately. Could she sense from her scent or touch that Angela was her mother?

Within a few seconds, however, she started to cry again. Angela was no longer producing milk to breast feed, so it was only a bottle of formula milk that would satisfy Maria's hunger now.

"Can you take her, please," Angela said, passing her back to me. "I don't know what to do."

The look of relief on her face when Maria was in my arms again spoke volumes.

"Don't worry, love," I reassured her. "It takes a while to learn how to look after a baby."

What I didn't mention, though, was that you have to want to do it in the first place. From what I had seen so far, there was no desire for that mother-and-baby bonding to occur.

"Maria's hungry, so I'll show you how to make her up a bottle," I said. "Let's take her downstairs and while I'm mixing up the formula milk, you can watch."

I demonstrated how to boil the bottle in a pan of hot water to make sure it was sterile, then mixed the correct quantity of formula powder with hot water, followed by cooling down the bottle in a jug of cold water before feeding baby Maria.

"This is how you test the temperature," I told her as I squirted milk from the teat on to our wrists. "Does that feel cool enough to drink yet?"

She nodded uncertainly, so I tested it myself.

"No, it's too hot still," I said. "That will burn the poor little mite's mouth. We'll wait another minute or so."

Picking up Maria from her moses basket, I sat down and rested her head in the crook of my arm.

"When we feed her, we have to make sure that she's not swallowing air with her milk," I said, tilting the bottle at the right angle. "Otherwise she'll get wind and that will hurt her little tummy."

Although Angela still seemed nervous, she watched with fascination as Maria glugged her milk.

"Would you like to have a try?" I asked. "I'll be right here if you want to hand her back, though."

"Okay," she said tentatively. "Let me see if I can do it right."

She found it difficult trying to hold Maria and feed her at the same time, but once I'd adjusted the bottle, she gradually got the hang of it. When Maria had finished feeding and I put her down in her cot for a nap, Angela's body language visibly relaxed.

As I put the kettle for another cuppa, she started to clear her throat.

"Thank you, Jeanie," she stammered. "I'm pleased Maria came to you. You've looked after her really well and now you're looking after me, too."

She paused and looked ashamed. I waited, not sure what was coming next.

"What I did was wrong, leaving Maria like that, wasn't it? I was afraid you'd think I was terrible for it."

I shook my head and smiled.

"No, Angela, I don't think that about you at all. You did the best you could in terrible circumstances. There aren't many girls your age who could have coped with what you had to do. Remember, none of what happened was your fault."

Angela's face fell and she stared despondently at the floor.

It was inevitable that flashbacks would haunt her, but I had no intention of pressing her for details.

Sitting next to her at the table, I gave her arm a comforting squeeze and said, "I know we've only just met, Angela, but whenever you need to talk, I'm here for you."

She gave me a small smile but said nothing.

The tension was broken by the sound of the front door suddenly being flung open and four sets of footsteps clattering into the hallway.

"We're home!" Bill called out, unnecessarily.

Angela looked nervous at the sound of this noisy invasion.

"Don't worry, love," I reassured her. "We're all very friendly. And my kids can't wait to meet you."

At that moment, Stevie's cheeky smiling face peered around the door, followed by Sarah and Sophie.

The three girls looked at each other in self-conscious silence until, after a few seconds, Sarah broke the ice.

"Wanna come to play in our room?" she asked. "We can play beauty salons. I've got a hairdryer, some proper rollers and a beauty kit."

Angela's face lit up.

"Go on, love," I said with an encouraging smile.

It seemed incongruous to watch this young girl, who had just been feeding and changing her baby, revert to a childlike world of play and make-believe.

"Tea will be ready in half an hour," I reminded Sarah as the three of them filed upstairs to the room she shared with Sophie and closed the door.

These days that bedroom door would have to be kept open. It's an official safeguarding rule, aimed at protecting minors. Whenever foster children play in the same bedroom as another child, there should be no closed doors.

Back then, however, no such rule existed, and in the space of a few minutes, Sarah and Sophie had both claimed Angela as their new special friend.

"I'm sitting next to Angela," Sophie declared when they came down for tea and made a dash for the kitchen table.

"Well I'm the eldest so I get first choice," countered Sarah, nudging her sister out of the way.

"Calm down, girls," laughed Bill, dishing out bowls of Irish stew while I sliced up a loaf of homemade bread and placed it on a plate at the centre of the table.

"One of you can sit opposite Angela and the other next to her. You can swap places at breakfast tomorrow."

"OK Dad," said Sarah, shooting Sophie an imperious look, while her sister screwed up her face and poked out her tongue.

Angela put her hand against her mouth to suppress a giggle, and this light-hearted atmosphere set the tone for the rest of our first meal together.

Although our guest seemed naturally shy, I could tell from her frequent smiles that she was happy to be with us. Sitting around a table as a family, a simple but important part of the day, was something she hadn't experienced for a very long time.

But how would she react if Maria suddenly started to cry and needed her nappy changed or a feed, I wondered? She was still just a child herself and the responsibility of looking after a baby 24 hours a day might well prove too much for her to take on.

Expecting her to look after Maria on her first night with us was a leap too far, so I kept the cot in my room for her middle of the night feed.

Despite her youth, Angela displayed a level of maturity which, I can only conclude, she must have gained when she was fending for herself at home.

After eating, she was the first one to jump up from the table to help clear away the dishes.

"Thank you for tea," she said, before heading upstairs with Sarah and Sophie to get ready for bed.

Bill and I looked at each other in pleasant surprise. Despite the horror of everything she had been through, Angela had not forgotten her manners.

However, her anger and pain were still bubbling away beneath the surface, as I discovered the next day.

After Bill had taken the kids to school, Angela and I had breakfast together in the kitchen.

She seemed subdued – gloomy even – as she munched on her toast and showed no interest whatsoever in Maria as I fed the baby her bottle.

"Is anything the matter, love?" I asked. "Are you feeling ill?"

Angela sipped her orange juice through a paper straw and didn't reply.

"Would you like to hold Maria?" I ventured. "She might need a cuddle soon."

Angela emphatically shook her head. This did not bode well.

Finally, she spoke.

"I miss my mum," she said, her voice trembling. "She left me, see. I suppose that's because she didn't love me, really. And then I left Maria, too. That makes me just as bad as my mum, doesn't it?"

It was sad to hear how this damaged girl had such a low opinion of herself

"Who told you that, Angela? Who told you that you're a bad person?" I asked.

She lowered her eyes in shame: she could hardly speak his name.

"My dad," she said. "He told me I'm bad like Mum."

"Listen to me, Angela," I said firmly. "You aren't bad or cruel. You're a young, frightened girl who got dragged into an awful situation that's not your fault.."

"It was my fault Mum left us!" she cried, her voice louder and more insistent. "Dad told me I had got between them, that ever since I was born Mum had ignored him."

What kind of heartless father would make his child feel responsible for his failed marriage after her mother had abandoned her?

"I'm going to be totally honest with you, Angela," I said, trying to keep my voice even. "Your parents – and they alone – are to blame for their relationship ending. They were very wrong and selfish to bring you into it.

"Your dad's behaviour towards you was a disgrace and he needs to take responsibility for that," I continued. "The authorities can deal with him while we help you to get back on your feet."

Suddenly, Angela stood up. "Can we put Maria in her cot upstairs please, Jeanie?" she asked. "I know she can't understand what we're saying, but I don't want to talk about this in front of her."

I understood Angela's reasoning completely. Here was her precious, innocent daughter whose life had only just begun, and already the atmosphere around her was being tainted by the ugly behaviour of Angela's parents.

"Yes, of course, love," I said, realising that I had probably taken the subject too far, too soon. "I'll take her up and put her down until her next feed. She needs her nap now anyway.

"By the way, Angela," I added as I passed her on my way out. "Maria's a gorgeous baby. She looks just like you."

When I returned, Angela was looking at a tattered black-and-white photograph. There was a bloodstained fingerprint on the back and it looked as if it had been ripped in half then pieced back together with sticky tape.

At first I assumed it was the photo of a Hollywood star. With her wavy dark hair and pale complexion, this glamorous woman beaming at the camera was the spitting image of a young Elizabeth Taylor.

Next to her, his face only half visible on the torn photo, was a tall, thin man with light hair and a carnation in his buttonhole.

It was a black-and-white picture so it was difficult to tell what colour the woman's eyes were, but judging by their shape and expression, they were just like Angela's.

"Who is this lady?" I asked, although I had already guessed the answer. "She's very beautiful."

A myriad of emotions flickered across Angela's face.

"That's my mum," she said with sadness and pride. "On her wedding day."

"Well, I can see the strong resemblance between you," I smiled. "And little Maria looks like you both."

At least her baby, with her dark hair and violet eyes, bore no resemblance to her dad – a similarity that would have made bonding with Maria practically impossible for Angela.

"Mum ran off with another man and left me with Dad," she said angrily. "So she obviously preferred that man to me."

"Yes, I was told by Janet and Carol about that, pet," I said softly. "That must have been horrendous, so upsetting for you."

Angela's eyes filled with tears.

"It wasn't the first time Mum walked out on us, though," she said. "She was always going off with one of her boyfriends, but she usually came back a few weeks later."

I hadn't realised until then that Kathleen had made a habit of deserting her child on a regular basis.

"When you say 'always going off', when did that start to happen?" I asked.

Angela looked embarrassed.

"Since I started at the big school," she murmured. "Mum would leave me with a neighbour and go out while Dad was at work.

Sometimes she'd stay out all night. Dad hit her once. I was in my bedroom and heard the furniture falling over. When they had fights I used to put my fingers in my ears and hide under the covers."

So Kathleen had neglected Angela since she was a little girl, preferring to go out on the town with her fellas than do ordinary things like taking her young daughter to the park.

When Angela got older, she became one of those so-called latch-key kids who let themselves in after school and had to fend for themselves. No wonder she seemed so capable now.

"So what did you have for your tea when you got home?" I asked. "Did your mum leave something for you to heat up?"

I had guessed the answer to that before Angela shook her head. "But I knew how to make toast," she said proudly. "And I would drink milk from the fridge. When Dad got in from work, he'd bring fish and chips or we'd have a can of tomato soup."

I could barely conceal my sadness for her, or anger towards her parents.

When Angela saw the look in my eye, she tried to defend her feckless mother.

"But Mum must have been sorry, really," she said, reciting the words as if she had told them to herself a thousand times before.

"Because when she came back, she always brought me lovely presents. Once she gave me a doll I'd always wanted – the one Dad had told me was too expensive. No-one in my class had that doll, only me."

So Kathleen would go out with one of her admirers who had a few quid, stay away from home for a few days, then return with a purse full of fivers and a lavish guilt gift. There was an obvious conclusion to make about the source of her income.

But it wasn't for me to sit in judgement. My role was to listen, support and, above all, to help Angela look after Maria.

"Mum always kissed me goodbye before she went out," Angela continued. "Except the last time."

She gazed down at her hands. "I waved to her through my bedroom window. She was getting into a really posh car and the old man opened the door for her."

"Did she wave back?" I asked, dreading her reply.

"No. She did look back, though, but I don't think she saw me. It was dark and the old man was telling her to hurry up. They drove off really fast."

So Kathleen had abandoned Angela for the last time without so much as a kiss or a wave goodbye. What kind of a mother does that? Kathleen was a classic narcissist, a self-obsessed, vain individual who didn't seem to care less about the daughter she had given birth to.

Yet Angela still loved her anyway.

"What are your favourite, happiest times with your mum?" I asked.

"When she took me with her to the hairdresser's and let me have my hair done at the same time as her," she recalled. "And when we watched nice films together and there was a lady who looked just like Mum in them."

So, two things that revolved around Kathleen's obvious obsession with her looks. I forced a smile to hide what I was really thinking.

But Angela did have one recollection of her mother that showed her in a surprisingly good light.

"Mum was good at looking after me when I was little," she said. "She used to be a nurse before she got married and whenever I was poorly, she always knew how to make me feel better straight away.

"She'd make me up a little bed on the sofa and tuck me inside the blankets. I put my head on a cushion in her lap and she'd stroke my forehead and sing me songs while we watched films."

At least Kathleen had shown her daughter some affection as she was growing up, a memory that Angela clung on to.

"I really thought she would come back again after she left last year," she said sadly. "I waited and waited for her. She always came home before. But this time she never did."

It defied belief how any mother could be so selfish and cruel.

"Is that why you tore her picture up, love?" I asked.

"No, not me! I didn't rip it," she said, evidently shocked at the mere idea. "Dad did it. After Mum disappeared again. I mended it with sticky tape and hid it in my room in case he tried to burn it."

"Whatever made you think he might do such a thing, Angela?" I asked.

"Because he threw all the nice gloves and dresses Mum left behind into the fire. He went mad."

It was hard to contemplate the fear and torment Angela's parents had put her through.

"Were you afraid of him?" I asked.

She nodded, her cheeks pinched white with pain.

"You don't have to tell me any more if you don't want to, love," I said.

But Angela had started now, and she wanted the whole truth to come out…

A Living Nightmare

"Dad used to drink a lot, especially after Mum left," said Angela. "He'd go to the pub after work and I wouldn't see him until the morning."

"So he left you on your own in the evening, then?"

"Yes, but I was fine on my own," she said. "I preferred it without Dad there because he was always angry and used to shout at me."

It seems that the longer Kathleen was away, the more her father turned his aggression towards her. When it became clear that Kathleen wouldn't return this time, his anger escalated.

"He smashed their wedding picture on the floor," Angela recalled, trembling at the memory. "The glass broke and he cut his hand. There was blood everywhere.

"Then he ripped up the photo and threw it away. After he went to bed, I crept out of my room, fished it out of the bin and stuck it back together.

"I hid it inside my wardrobe in case Dad found it and burned that, too. It's the only picture I've got of Mum. I wanted to keep it in case I forget what she looks like. It's all I have left of her now."

Angela's recollection of how her own mother had abandoned her was heartbreaking enough. But then came the harrowing account of how she suffered at the hands of her father.

Biting her bottom lip, Angela clenched her hands until her knuckles turned white as she described to me what happened a few months after Kathleen's abrupt departure.

"I was in bed asleep when Dad came home drunk again," she whispered. "He was shouting for Mum, calling her horrible names and swearing. Then I heard him stumbling around on the landing outside my room. I was scared so I hid under my sheets. I thought he was going to hit me like he used to hit her."

She paused and closed her eyes as if to blank out the memory of what occurred next.

"Dad bashed open my bedroom door. He started calling me Kathleen and crying, then he pulled the covers off me. He slapped my face and punched me in the tummy."

Her words fell like blows as I heard the details of the horrific attack on that delicate young girl in front of me.

I reached out and held Angela's hand, summoning up all my self-control to remain outwardly calm as she went on to tell me what that monster said and did to her that night.

Yanking her from her bed, he dragged her into his bedroom and threw her onto the bed he had shared with his wife.

"You're a filthy whore, Kathleen!" he hissed, breathing foul whisky fumes into his daughter's face. "Nothing but a slut."

Angela told me how, rigid with fear, she screamed for her mother, but even that didn't bring her father to his senses.

He raped that defenceless child – his own daughter – before passing out in a heap on the bed next to her.

Despite feeling traumatised and in pain, Angela ran herself a warm bath and washed away the blood. He had hurt her badly. She started her periods a few months earlier, so she wore a sanitary towel to stop the blood from staining her sheets and clothes.

To avoid bumping into her father the next morning, Angela left early for school, soothing the red marks on her cheeks with a cold wet flannel and camouflaging them with a dab of her mother's face powder.

The school was the only place where Angela felt safe.

"Did you tell anyone at all what had happened, love?" I asked. "A best friend?"

"I started to," she said, tears streaming down her face. "When one of my friends asked me about the mark on my face. She could tell that they were fingerprints. When I told her my dad did it, she moved away from me, as if I had something wrong with me. After that, I was afraid to tell anyone."

For months Angela avoided her father as much as possible, retreating to her room at night and barricading the door with a dressing table she had managed to drag across the room in front of it. But he never attempted to attack her again, sinking instead into a constant drunken stupor and passing out in his room.

"It was good when that happened," said Angela. "Without him around, I could go into the kitchen to make my meals and sleep properly at night."

Her peace of mind was short-lived.

When she missed her next period and started suffering from morning sickness, she realised that she must be pregnant, but she didn't dare tell a soul.

"I was scared of what might happen to me. If they put Dad in prison, where would I live? I didn't even have a mum to look after me any more."

"It must have been hard going to school and hiding it from everyone," I said.

"I had to rush out of the classroom to be sick a lot," she recalled. "I pretended that I had a tummy upset or had started my period. After I'd thrown up in the cubicle, I'd splash my face with cold water and go back into class."

I empathised with Angela more than she would ever know.

"I expect you started wearing baggy clothes to cover your bump, didn't you, love? Skirts with elasticated waists and tops a few sizes too big?"

She nodded.

"I'm quite thin really and my school uniform was already too big for me. So when my tummy started growing, it didn't show much at first. My blouse is baggy, too, and that covered up my top part. But when I couldn't hide my bump any more I stopped going to school."

"Was there really no-one you could turn to, Angela?" I asked. "A grandmother or an aunt? A kind neighbour?"

She shook her head. "I was too scared. I thought that if I talked about what had happened, Dad would get into trouble. I wasn't sure what would happen to me then."

Without a soul in the world to help, Angela gave birth on her own in the bathroom at home while her father was out getting drunk.

"It really hurt," she told me, shuddering at the memory. "I thought I was dying."

But what young Angela did singlehandedly in a bathtub of warm water and with a pair of nail scissors, was extraordinary.

"You were very brave, love," I told her. "Not many women or girls could go through with that on their own. You're stronger than you think, you know."

She looked at me in surprise.

"Do you really think so, Jeanie?"

"From what I've seen and heard so far, I know so," I said firmly.

After the relief of telling me her story, Angela started to sob and I put my arms around her. "What am I going to do, Jeanie?" she asked desperately, her voice muffled against my shoulder. "I've got no Mum, my dad's going to prison, and now I have a little baby to look after. I can't do it, I can't."

It was a daunting picture, to be sure, but I knew that if Angela still had half the grit and gumption it took for her to come through this nightmare, there was a good chance she could cope with what lay ahead.

"Listen to me, Angela," I said soothingly. "We're going to take small steps and manage one day at a time. Yes, you're only 15, but you aren't the first teenage girl to have a baby and you certainly won't be the last.

"I can't tell you not to worry or promise that it's going to be easy. The truth is, love, that being a mother is a full-on job that requires toughness as well as a lot of love. I think you can do it – but only if you want to.

"You're still very young with your whole life ahead of you. At the end of the day, whether or not you keep Maria is entirely your decision. No-one will judge you for the choice you make."

Catching her breath, Angela looked at me with an expression of relief.

"I can promise you this, young lady," I continued. "As long as you and Maria are under my roof, I will be with you all the way. I'll fight tooth and nail for you both, as if you were my own. And I know Bill would promise the same."

Angela stared at me, her eyes shining. "Thanks Jeanie," she smiled. "I don't think I've ever had someone fight for me before."

Now it was my turn to feel overcome with emotion, but I knew I had to stay strong for Angela.

At that moment it was Maria, not me, who began to cry.

It was time for her next nappy change and feed, and as I quickly climbed the stairs to attend to her, Angela followed.

Although she seemed more relaxed with Maria now, she was understandably still nervous about holding her.

"Could she grow to love this child?" I wondered, as Angela declined to give Maria her bottle, preferring to watch me do it instead.

A week later, things had barely changed. Although Angela knew by then how to change Maria's nappies and make up a bottle of formula milk, she would rush off to play with Sarah and Sophie as soon as they came home from school.

I had to remind myself that she was, after all, barely more than a child herself.

When I made notes in my log book at the end of every day – an important record that foster carers must keep – I reported the facts accurately for the sake of both Angela and her baby.

Even if she decided that she wanted to keep Maria, there was no way I could recommend this without evidence of her ability and wholehearted commitment.

However, when Carol and Janet made an appointment for what I assumed to be a weekly assessment, the situation took an unexpected turn.

"Jeanie, we have some news about Angela's mother," said Carol, after Janet asked Angela to take her upstairs to see Maria, an excuse to observe her interaction with her baby.

From what I'd understood so far, Kathleen had disappeared for good with her fancy man, but when I saw the serious expression on Carol's face, I assumed the worst.

"So that fella she went off with turned out to be as bad as her husband?" I asked, afraid of what she was going to tell me next.

I dreaded to think how Angela would react if some terrible ill had befallen her mum. "Is she all right? Did he hurt her?"

"No, not physically," replied Carol. "But he was very controlling."

"How do we know this?"

"The police managed to track her down after they took Angela's dad in for questioning," explained Carol. "When they told her what he had done to Angela, she was devastated."

I shook my head and rolled my eyes.

"So she should be," I said. "She left that girl for over a year, without so much as sending her a letter or a birthday card. Yet Angela still idolises her."

Carol listened and nodded, but as she continued to fill me in, I discovered that all was not as it seemed.

During a meeting with social services, Kathleen had given her account of why she left, casting a fresh light on the sorry situation.

"She claims that throughout their marriage, her husband was a very jealous, aggressive, paranoid man," Carol explained. "Kathleen's an attractive woman, but if a man so much as glanced in her direction, he would blame her for it.

"She says that he accused her of encouraging it, of giving men the eye. As time went on, he became convinced that she was being unfaithful. He used to call her a whore and started hitting her in front of Angela."

Although I felt some sympathy for Kathleen, I couldn't forget what she and her husband had made Angela suffer, with no care for how their disintegrating marriage would affect her.

"Did Kathleen try to get help?" I asked. "Surely she could have left him and taken Angela to live with her mother, or something? Leaving her there on her own with a violent father was unforgivable."

Carol shook her head.

That didn't surprise me in the slightest. In the Catholic community where I grew up, this was the standard instruction given by priests to battered wives desperate for help.

But if her husband really had been imagining that she was unfaithful, why did she go on to prove his suspicions to be true?

"We think the emotional and physical abuse finally pushed her over the edge and away," explained Carol. "She saw it as her only way out."

"And into the arms of more sympathetic and appreciative men, I suppose," I concluded.

But that still didn't explain adequately to me why Kathleen agreed to a midnight flit with her lover when it meant leaving her young daughter at the mercy of her volatile father? For me, personally, that was inexcusable – as was choosing her lover over her child.

However, in my professional capacity it wasn't for me to judge.

"Kathleen claims that her man-friend whisked her away before she'd even had the chance to say goodbye to Angela," said Carol. "After that, he tried to stop her from getting in touch. He was a dominating type who used his money to get his own way.

"Mind you, she insists that she sent Angela birthday and Christmas cards. She put money inside, too."

Yet Angela had been adamant that since she left, her mother had made no contact with her whatsoever. The only explanation was that her father had hidden the cards from her – and kept the cash for himself.

Poor Angela, abandoned by her mother, then raped and deceived by her father. She deserved far better parents than them.

Yet, Carol went on to tell me, Kathleen was keen to come back into her daughter's life.

"When she found out what had happened, she blamed herself. She wanted to see Angela straight away and bring her to live with her and her fella. But he wouldn't accept Angela and told her she had to choose between them."

"No prizes for guessing who she picked," I scoffed.

"She didn't hesitate," said Carol. "She chose Angela."

I raised my eyebrows in surprise.

"Well that's a turn-up for the books," I gasped. "Does she mean it, though? And what about the baby? Does she want to take Maria on too, knowing what her husband did?"

Carol hesitated.

"We're not sure yet," she said. "She's still thinking that part through. But we've no intention of letting Angela – or Maria – go anywhere until we're convinced there's a stable home waiting for them."

Carol told me that Kathleen had already broken up with her controlling fella and moved back into the flat, making it ready for Angela's return. To erase painful memories, she had started to transform it, ripping out the soiled carpets and moving all the furniture around to prepare for a fresh start.

"What were her reasons for not wanting to see Maria yet?" I asked.

In fact, the answer to that question was pretty obvious.

This innocent babe would be a constant reminder of what Angela's father had done to her. A commitment to bringing her up with love was a pledge that could not be made lightly.

"At the end of the day, we have to shelve our personal thoughts and feelings about Kathleen and her husband," said Carol. "Our priorities are Angela and her baby, and putting their welfare first."

It wasn't common practice for my opinion to be asked regarding where a child should live after I had fostered them, except in extreme cases. I was once asked if I thought a youngster should live with her mother or her father, who had separated. I suggested her father as, unlike her mother, he was reliable, dependable and would provide for her. My assessment proved to be correct, as that little girl grew up in a stable home.

All these years later, I'm pleased to have made that call – even though immediately after the decision was made, I was afraid that the furious, volatile mother would physically attack me as I drove her in my car away from the meeting.

But it is my belief that the voice of the child should always be heard loudest.

"What if Angela doesn't even want to see her mum?" I asked.

"We would never force Angela to do anything she doesn't want to do, Jeanie," Carol assured me. "If she does want to meet her mum, we'll arrange for them to see each other in a neutral place, with a social worker – probably Janet – present. That way we can assess how they get on and if we think it will work between them."

When Angela came back downstairs with Janet, Carol explained that they had found her mother and that she was keen to see her.

I'll never forget the look of surprise and relief in Angela's eyes. "When?" she gasped. "Today?"

The reunion was arranged to take place at a contact centre the following afternoon, but I noted with a sinking feeling that Kathleen had only requested to see her daughter – not baby Maria.

This detail had not occurred to Angela, though: all she could think about was that her mum, who she still adored, wanted her.

As she got ready to go, the poor girl's demeanour changed. Suddenly she was sick with nerves. And doubt.

"What if she changes her mind, Jeanie?" she asked, as she slipped on her coat. "What if she goes off and leaves me again?"

The same fear had crossed my mind, but I didn't let my reservations show.

"First things first, love," I said cheerfully. "Try not to worry about any of that for now. See how you get on – and then you can have a little think about whether you're ready to go back and live with your mum. Talk to me about it, if you want.

"And remember," I added as Janet rang the doorbell to pick her up. "I'll support whatever you decide."

When Angela returned a few hours later, she was elated. Beaming with joy and brimming with an energy I hadn't seen in her since she had come to live with us, she bounded upstairs.

Was she popping in to take a quick peek at Maria in her cot?

From the direction of her footsteps on the landing, no, she had gone into her room and I could hear the muffled sound of her rifling through her chest of drawers.

I looked at Janet. The expression on her face was solemn, far more sombre than usual.

"Can I speak to you in private, please, Jeanie?" she asked quietly.

"Sure," I said, leading her through to the kitchen and shutting the door behind us. "Angela seems very... happy. I assume it all went well with her mum, then?"

She hesitated, as if trying to formulate an answer.

"Well, yes," she said, quickly adding, "and no."

Somehow I knew what was coming next.

"There's no doubt that Angela's excited about living with her mum," she said. "And Kathleen seems serious about it all, she was very affectionate with her, told her how sorry she was for leaving her. There were tears on both sides, and promises about how everything will be different this time around, too.

"We'll arrange another meeting between them," she continued. "Just to make sure it's consistent, that they both want it."

Yet one important name was missing from Janet's appraisal.

"What about Maria?" I asked. "Did they talk about her, too?"

Janet paused and nodded.

"We discussed Maria with Kathleen ahead of her meeting with Angela," she said, lowering her voice. "I'm afraid she doesn't want to see her."

My heart sank.

"What, never?" I asked incredulously. "Won't she even consider it?"

Janet gave a brief shake of the head.

"So she'll only take Angela back without Maria?" I said, unable to conceal my indignation.

With regret in her voice, Janet whispered a barely discernible "Yes."

"But that puts Angela in a terrible position," I protested. "It means she'll have to choose between her mother and her baby!"

It was a tough – and tragic – scenario, but with many more miles on the clock in this business than me, Janet had seen it all before.

"Kathleen has made her decision, Jeanie. And she assures us she won't change her mind on that score."

A tense silence fell between us as I processed the implications.

"What about Angela?" I asked softly. "Does she know about this yet?"

Janet nodded.

"And what did she say about giving up Maria? She's hardly had a chance to bond with her yet."

I couldn't believe that Kathleen would reject that beautiful grandaughter before she had even seen her – or that Angela would make such a choice without thinking it through for a while first.

"Angela's still just a child herself," said Janet. "She's a very nice girl, but let's be honest – she's not shown much promise in taking on the demands of motherhood, has she?"

Although Janet was right on that count, I felt sad that Maria was about to be left behind for the second time in her short life.

"Try not to see this as an abandonment, Jeanie," reasoned Janet. "Maria will be adopted by a family who will love and care for her wholeheartedly. She'll grow up in a secure home – without the danger of ever finding out how she was conceived.

"Meanwhile, Angela can go back to school and get on with her life. She can heal the rift with her mum. Believe me, I think this is the most sensible outcome for everyone."

I nodded in resignation, but inside I was struggling to come to terms with it all.

After Janet had left, I looked at little Maria asleep in her cot, oblivious to her fate, and felt a pang in my heart.

"You will be loved," I whispered. "I promise you that."

Pulling myself together, I tip-toed out.

I could still hear a flurry of activity inside Angela's room, so I tapped on the door.

"Come in," she called, her voice lighter and more cheerful than I had ever heard it.

As I gently opened the door, I saw her suitcase open on the bed and she was systematically filling it with her few clothes and belongings.

"Oh, I didn't think you needed to pack yet, love," I said. "Don't you have another meeting with your mum first?"

"Yes," she said, glancing up. "But I want to be ready for when I go home."

Angela was clearly overjoyed at the prospect of living with her mum again, despite her baby not being part of that unit.

"Mum wants me back, Jeanie. I thought she'd gone because she didn't really love me. But this proves that she does, doesn't it?"

"It certainly looks that way, pet," I said, suppressing my own doubts.

At that moment, Maria began to cry for her feed, but instead of dashing off to attend to her as I usually would, I stopped in my tracks.

Would Angela respond and the urge to care for her baby finally kick in? Would the sound of her daughter crying out penetrate her bubble and remind her of the other person that needed to be considered?

It was not to be – the sound barely registered with her.

In that split second, her response had told me exactly what I needed to know: Angela was not ready to be a mother. She had made the right decision.

A few days later, Janet arrived to take Angela home, where her mum Kathleen was waiting for her.

Although Maria was far too young to understand what was happening, I was relieved that she was asleep when it was time for Angela to say goodbye.

Leaning over the cot, she kissed her slumbering baby gently on the forehead.

"I'm sorry," she whispered to Maria, who was blissfully oblivious and making sweet snuffling sounds.

There were tears in my eyes when Angela stood up and left the room to get her things together for her new life. I watched her as she walked back into the room.

"Be happy, little one," she whispered, giving her baby one last look as she made for the door with a fresh lightness in her step. Without even looking back this time, she walked out of Maria's life forever.

We were all upset by Angela's decision, and I wondered if she would change her mind and come back for her baby.

A week later, however, Janet called to explain that they'd found a family who were keen to adopt Maria and that was that.

We said our goodbyes. I must admit I shed a few more tears as I held that gorgeous little girl for the last time. I would miss those bottle feeds: her warm weight on my chest, the sweet milky scent of her and her violet eyes gazing trustingly at mine. But I had no doubts that she was going to a secure place where she would be loved. Over the years, I would never say goodbye to a little one without a tiny pang, but this first one was the hardest.

"I'd better put the cot back into the loft," said Bill sadly. "No point leaving it there, taking up space."

"Yes, I know, love," I replied. "We've no use for it now."

I watched as he methodically dismantled what had become Maria's cot, re-packed it in its box and put it back into the eaves.

However, it turned out that we would be needing it back down again sooner than we thought.

Susan

It was a sunny spring morning and a blackbird was singing in the may tree outside our bedroom window when I heard the phone ring.

With a tired groan, Bill pulled the pillow over his head and mumbled, "No peace for the wicked!"

I glanced at the alarm clock on the bedside table. It was 8am, a rare lie-in for us because the kids were on half term, so Bill had taken a few days off too.

I ambled downstairs in my nightie.

"Hello," I croaked.

"Morning, Jeanie," chimed the familiar voice of our link worker Carol. "I hope I haven't woken you up? I can call back later if you like?"

"No, it's fine," I replied, clearing my throat in an effort to sound more alert. "I'll be wide awake in a sec."

Carol's laugh tinkled down the phone.

"How have you all been since Angela and baby Maria left?" she asked. "I know how fond you were of them."

I glanced at Maria's neatly folded white blanket, which had been left behind accidentally.

"OK. How's Maria's settling in with her new family?" I asked.

"She's thriving," said Carol. "Janet saw her last week and says her adoptive parents dote on her. Well, she's such a bonny little thing, looks more like her mum than ever, I'm told."

A lump formed in my throat.

I often wondered – and still do to this day – if Angela would ever regret her irreversible decision to give up her little baby. I hoped not...

"How is Angela?" I asked tentatively.

While I had no doubt that Maria would be placed with parents who would love and care for her, I felt uneasy about Angela's future with her own mother.

Had Kathleen given her the level of love and security she had promised?

"Oh, don't worry on that score," enthused Carol. "Angela's doing well and seems very happy. She's back at school now, too.

"And she didn't have to go to court. Her dad admitted what he'd done and received a custodial sentence. Not a long one, mind you. But even when he's let out, he's banned from going near her or Kathleen. So Angela's safe."

I let out a sigh of relief.

"How is the set-up at home with her mum?" I asked.

Carol paused.

"Well, that was never going to be easy," she began, "but it's heading in the right direction. Kathleen had a lot of personal changes to make, but she seems to have finally got her priorities right. I hear she's trying to be a good mum."

She stopped and gave a wry little laugh.

"Mind you, Jeanie, she's still a bit of a vain so-and-so," she said. "She won't let anyone into the flat unless she's put her lipstick on first!"

"Well there's a surprise," I chuckled.

Kathleen's vanity aside, this was a happy ending of sorts for both Angela and Maria.

"All credit to you, Jeanie," said Carol. "You did a great job. Angela and Maria might not have reached where they are now without you."

My spirits soared. From the ashes of damage and devastation, Angela was healing her emotional wounds while Maria had begun a new life with parents who had made her the centre of their world.

However, as I discovered further on down the line, not every case that came your way would end on such a positive note.

In reality, there are seldom fairytale endings – just people making the best of difficult situations. People like Susan, my new foster case...

"This young girl is much more of a challenge than Angela," warned Carol. "But I'm hoping you might be able to help her."

She explained that Susan was a 15-year-old girl in care, who had fallen pregnant while being looked after at a children's home. She was only six weeks away from her due date and my task would be to see her through the birth and show her how to look after her baby.

It would be a huge commitment.

"You'd better come over and tell me all about her," I said.

Twenty minutes later, Carol was sitting on my sofa with a cup of tea, filling me in on Susan's tragic and desperately disturbing background.

Brought up in a squalid flat on an estate hardly fit for habitation, Susan had been severely neglected by her parents, who were both addicts.

"She's a vulnerable child, from what we would describe as an abusive background," Carol explained. "Mind, you wouldn't think she was that vulnerable if you heard her language. She shouts and swears, and likes to throw her weight around."

I raised my eyebrows.

Carol continued: "We need a foster mother – hopefully you – to guide her through the rest of the pregnancy and the birth."

"So she's keeping the child, then" I asked. "Do you think she's got it in her to look after a kid?"

"At the moment, no. We're not even sure if she wants to keep it yet. Either way, we thought you'd be the best person to help her, then show her how to look after her baby, like you did with Angela.

"Susan's had a very unfortunate start in life, I'm afraid. Her dad's a violent alcoholic and her mum's addicted to alcohol and valium.

"The father was a heavy drinker before she was born, but his sessions at the pub escalated after he lost his job down the docks."

"He found the cash for his booze though, didn't he?" I said.

Carol nodded: "Susan's mum, Hannah, had a few pounds stashed away in a drawer. But he found it and stole it from her. She needed that money for an emergency like this, but she was scared of him."

His drunken temper sounded horrific.

"He was always brawling down the pub or in the street," said Carol. "And he used to knock Hannah around, force her to have sex with him, sometimes in front of Susan. We think he was violent towards Susan, too."

"Did her mum ever report him?" I asked. "Get the police involved?"

"A neighbour called 999 a few times, but when the police turned up, they classed it a 'domestic'. All they did was tell Susan's dad to sober up, then leave Susan and her mum at his mercy."

It was a sad and all too familiar sorry state of affairs. If a man attacked his wife and kids, the police rarely intervened in those days.

Incredible as it may seem now, there was no law against men raping their wives back then. It was thought that women waived their right to consent when they made their wedding vows. Besides, women and girls were viewed as property, belonging first to their fathers, then to their husbands.

There was a lot of victim blaming, too. When a child had been beaten by his dad, some people would defend his attacker.

"That kid was naughty; he was a cheeky little sod," was a common justification, or "She answered back; she deserved it."

That insidious attitude persisted in communities where everyone knew a man was beating, or even raping, his wife.

"She provoked him," was a favourite get-out clause, along with "She should have had his tea on the table in time! No wonder he gave her a good hiding."

As a child it seemed confusing to me that even when this tea, a symbol of her love and obedience, had been prepared, a man could still be excused for whacking his wife.

"Well, what did you expect?" I heard a matronly older woman tell her daughter on their way home from church. This young woman was weeping and nursing a black eye from her "caring" new husband.

From what I could gather, he had stayed out all night and she had, quite reasonably, asked him where he had been and why he hadn't come home for the tea she had spent all day preparing for him.

"You shouldn't have shouted at him," her mother snapped. "He's the head of the household, you need to learn that. Besides, you've let yourself go since he put that ring on your finger. He'll start looking elsewhere if you don't pull your socks up, my girl."

When families protect an abuser in their midst, their victims don't stand a chance.

"I suppose Susan's mum didn't leave because there was nowhere to go," I said. "And no money to pay the rent even if she did have the courage to get out."

Walking out on your husband wasn't socially acceptable – or even possible – back then. How could a woman leave when she had no support within her own community and no money of her own?

I recalled how some of the wives around where I grew up in Ireland would suffer in silence at the hands of drunken, violent husbands.

Even the church refused to be their sanctuary. Our priest would tell the women who confided in him that they had to endure the abuse – despite the fact it also endangered their kids – and put their sacred marriage vows first.

"Pray that it will get better," he would advise in that irritatingly calm, patronising tone, while some poor woman with a black eye was standing in front of him, pleading for help. And if she then turned up to Mass with a cut on her lip and her arm in a sling, the priest must have presumed she hadn't prayed hard enough.

Instead of turning to a priest, Hannah consulted a doctor, and his assistance was as bad as any priest's.

When she told him about the regular beatings she endured from her husband, the GP diagnosed depression and repeatedly prescribed her valium, a highly addictive drug. The consequences proved damaging, not only for her, but also for her child.

After knocking back the valium when she should have been making her daughter's breakfast, Hannah would have a few sherries to take the edge off her miserable life, too. It was a toxic combination.

Susan's life at home became more unstable than ever. Her parents were so volatile and too caught up in their own problems to think, or even care, about her needs.

From the moment Susan woke up to the time she went to bed, her intoxicated parents were either collapsed or stumbling over the furniture.

The worst scenario was witnessing her dad knock her mum around like a pin ball, or forcing his sweaty, heaving body on top of her. That's when Susan would run off to her room and hide under the covers.

"Poor kid," I said, shaking my head in anger. "God knows what damage it caused to witness all that. Couldn't anyone else in the family have stepped in to stop it?"

I'm a firm believer in the importance of grandparents in children's lives. Their stability, wisdom and kindness is invaluable, and they offer another dimension of love and nurturing to help young ones thrive.

Sadly, this support network was not available to Susan: both sets of grandparents lived far away in Northern Ireland. And in any case, one of her grandparents may not have been such a positive influence.

"From what I gather, her paternal grandfather was an alcoholic, too," said Carol. "So that's the kind of role model her dad grew up with. He thinks his behaviour's normal."

Despite raising the alarm in a visit to her doctor, Susan's mother was ignored. Like many women in the same boat, she didn't have the economic power – her own money – to support and save herself and her child.

"The family ended up living in squalor," continued Carol. "Neither parent was ever in a fit state long enough to clean their council flat.

The worst of it, though, was their neglect of Susan. She was existing on little more than bread and jam by the time social services got to her."

"So who raised the alarm?" I asked.

"The school stepped in first," explained Carol. "When Susan started playing truant, a teacher went round to the flat. Up until then she'd done a very good job of hiding her home life from her teachers and classmates."

As I've learned over the years, children often protect their dysfunctional families for a variety of reasons – fear of being blamed, being separated from siblings, or their parents being sent to prison, and out of misplaced loyalty or embarrassment.

It's often the devil they know that wins, and even the worst abused kids find their connection to their abusive parents hard to break or betray.

Susan managed to protect her parents by keeping her secret. She became a loner and rarely made friends.

"To be honest, the other kids probably kept their distance because of the smell, too," said Carol. "The poor girl's hygiene was way off because she had no money for deodorant, sanitary pads, or even soap. And she gave up trying to wash her clothes in the sink so they were always dirty."

"So what happened when the teacher confronted Susan's parents, what was their explanation for her dropping out of school?" I asked.

"They were both crashed out and in no fit state to speak," she said. "It looked like a drugs den. As for the smell… the place was filthy."

I cringed when she told me how, as well as empty booze bottles and broken glass scattered over every surface, there were stale urine and excrement stains all over the carpets.

"Susan was so ashamed, she couldn't look her teacher in the eye," said Carol. "The only room in the flat that was remotely clean was her tiny bedroom."

My heart went out to the poor kid.

Despite her hostile environment at home, Susan's teachers maintained that she was a bright girl who showed academic promise.

"It's difficult to believe when you meet her now," said Carol, "but she used to be a shy girl who loved reading and was good at writing stories."

Retreating into a world of fantasy was Susan's escape.

How many other youngsters out there, I wondered, had created the façade that they were leading normal lives while frantically covering up for their abusive parents.

I thought I'd heard the worst of Susan's plight, but there was more to come.

"As soon as the teacher saw Susan at her flat, she understood why she'd suddenly stopped going to school," explained Carol. "She was black and blue, with bruises on her arms and face. She couldn't cover them up, you see."

I gasped. "Who'd knocked her about? Her dad?"

"We still don't know," said Carol. "When social services got involved, she refused to talk about it. She's blocked the bad memories out.

"But there were all manner of alcoholics and dodgy characters going into the flat. It could have been any of them."

I shook my head: this was an unbelievably sad story.

Carol lowered her voice to continue.

"There's another terrible aspect to this, Jeanie. We think Susan's dad might even have been pimping his wife out for cash..."

A dark thought flitted through my mind.

"Surely not Susan too?"

"It's possible," she whispered.

As a gloomy silence fell between us, I thought about all the horrors Susan must have suffered. It explained why, as Carol suggested, she had put up a protective wall of either silence or aggression.

But there was another key player in this sordid tangled web who hadn't been named yet – the baby's father.

"Who is he?" I asked Carol. "Don't tell me..."

"No, not her father, nothing like that this time. Susan was definitely not pregnant when she arrived at the home a year ago.

"We suspect the father is a young man called Mark, a bit of a waster, really, a petty criminal who she started hanging around with in the town. So far she's refused to confirm it, though."

I was shocked that the children's home had failed to keep Susan safe.

"The care workers couldn't keep tabs on her for 24 hours a day," said Carol. "Whenever they tried to give her a curfew or reason with her, she'd laugh in their faces."

Since becoming a foster mum I've learnt that children from abusive backgrounds react differently to the experiences they've endured.

While Angela had retreated into her shell and become quiet and withdrawn, Susan ended up choosing the opposite path. From being a shy, conscientious girl at school, she had transformed into a loud, uncontrollable rebel and a bully.

"She became prone to angry outbursts and temper tantrums," said Carol. "A lot of the kids – and even some of the workers in the children's home – are afraid of her."

Highly volatile and unpredictable, she would let rip. Suddenly kicking off made her feel powerful rather than helpless, and got her the attention she had previously lacked.

"She discovered that by being aggressive and making other youngsters afraid of her, she could get her own way," said Carol. "Sometimes she'd even pretend to be angry in order to manipulate people."

Her behaviour deteriorated after she started mixing with a group of older boys who used to hang around the town.

"They're well known in the area for thieving and robbing," said Carol. "They lurk on park benches and bum around the shops, looking for victims to fleece.

"After she'd been with these lads, she would return to the home with bottles of expensive perfume, make-up and jewellery in her pocket that she couldn't possibly have afforded to buy herself. "The worst of it was the revealing clothes. Short skirts, see-through tops, all completely inappropriate for a girl of her age. Then she'd deliberately flaunt it all in front of us, as if to say, 'There's nothing you can do about it.'"

"Perhaps she stole the items to prove herself, to be part of the gang?" I suggested. "Maybe she wanted to show she could pilfer, too, to gain some kudos among them?"

Carol shook her head.

"One of the care workers actually saw Mark, the gang leader, hand her a bracelet when he dropped her off outside the home in his car," she said. "We think he was the one sweetening her up with presents – probably stolen goods – either in exchange for sex or passing her around to his mates for money."

It was becoming clear to me, now.

This vulnerable girl had been taken advantage of and had fallen into a trap that was closely akin to prostitution. These young men – all over the age of 18 – should have been brought to account for having sex with an underage youngster.

"She's a big girl, I know," said Carol. "And she looks older than she really is, especially when she's plastering on the make-up. But whoever got her pregnant must have known she was still a kid."

When she missed a period, panic-stricken Susan told no-one. She plunged into a state of denial, hiding her bump under big skirts until it was too late to consider her options.

I was 18 years old – just a few years older than Susan – when I fell pregnant, and so I understood exactly how lost, lonely and scared that poor girl must have felt underneath all her bravado. I really felt for her.

"So have the police approached this gang of lads to find out who did this to her?" I asked. "Susan's underage; whoever it was broke the law."

"We tried that, Jeanie," said Carol, sighing in frustration. "Although the police questioned the gang's ringleader, Mark, he denied everything.

"Then, when they spoke to Susan, she refused to answer any of their questions. So we couldn't prove a thing.

"And," she added, "I think that because of her defiant attitude, the police didn't regard her as an underage innocent girl.

"When they looked at her, they just saw a wilful, out-of -control delinquent who knew exactly what she was doing and had brought it all – including the pregnancy – upon herself.

"In fact, as the two policemen were leaving, Janet overheard one of them, the youngest, use the word 'tart'. She pulled him up on it, of course, verbally savaged him."

I was livid.

What was happening under the noses of the authorities is now known as grooming. In those days, however, women and girls were often blamed for sexual crimes committed against them – and sadly in some cases they still are.

"The sad fact is, she's probably still having sex with that lad – and possible other lads – who got her into this state in the first place," said Carol. "Although she's expecting a baby, she's out of control. We've tried telling her she's risking her health – and that of the baby   but she won't listen."

I felt a combination of sympathy and alarm.

Susan was a young girl, not much older than my daughter Sarah.

By allowing herself to be degraded, passed around from man to man, she was committing an act of self-harm. Most of all, however, it was a criminal offence that should have sent Mark and his low-life mates to jail.

Although she was cynically being bought and sold, she probably considered these sordid encounters to be affection, something that had rarely featured in her life before.

After the lack of love and neglect that led her to being placed in care in the first place, her hunger for attention, any kind of attention, had led to her getting pregnant.

As I learned throughout years of fostering, for some girls, any flattery from the opposite sex, however underhand the intention, makes them feel wanted.

If I was going to foster Susan, I would need to keep any undesirable influences away, not only from her, but also from my family.

"Can we make sure that this Mark and his mob won't know where we live?" I asked Carol. "We can't have him hanging around outside the house. Or even worse, forcing his way in."

"We can try," Susan nodded. "We won't tell Susan your address, and once she's settled in, she'll spend every day with you, preparing for the birth. She won't leave your side, so she won't have a chance to hang around with Mark."

I paused for a second to consider the demands that would be made with Susan in our midst.

What she needed most was a calm environment, a proper family routine and someone to see her through the final stages of her pregnancy – and beyond.

Could I take this on, knowing the dangers and complications it would entail?

"Has Susan said whether she wants to keep the baby?" I asked. "She's very young and from what you've said, Carol, her behaviour suggests she may not be mature enough yet to be a mum."

Carol shrugged.

"We don't know the answer to that yet," she said. "But while she – and we – are deciding, we have to make sure that when the baby's born, she looks after it properly. She'll need a lot of maternal guidance from you for that, Jeanie. If you decided to take her on, that is."

Considering Susan's disturbing background, there was a lot to think about.

"I'll need to speak to Bill and the kids first, Carol," I said. "But if we go ahead, it sounds like we're in for a bumpy ride!"

"I understand, Jeanie," she smiled. "Everyone needs to be on the same page and fully on board. If there's any doubt, let me know."

Over tea that evening, I discussed Susan with Bill and the kids.

I explained that not only would we be looking after a troubled teen under our roof, we would also be helping her through the birth of a baby and helping her to be a mum.

Hearing the words "teenage girl", Sarah's face lit up with excitement.

"At last, someone more my own age to hang out with," she said, looking pointedly at Sophie and Stevie. "We can talk about music, make-up and fashion. Grown-up stuff."

I needed to impress upon all three that it was unlikely Susan would be the fluffy, playful young girl they imagined.

Although I dreaded having to disappoint them with the truth, this frank discussion is a necessary part of fostering and there could be no glossing over the problems we would inevitably face if Susan moved in.

"Susan is quite different to Angela," I explained as three pairs of wide eyes searched my face for clues as to what I meant. "She might not be interested in playing the same games as you. She's having a baby soon so she'll probably be very tired – and grumpy." Sarah and Sophie looked disappointed, whereas Stevie shrugged and carried on eating his tea.

"But once you get to know Susan, she might open up," I added with an encouraging smile. "We'll have to give her time to adjust, to get used to us all. It must be quite scary to be faced with us lot!"

Presenting our family – not Susan – as the scary element diffused the situation and made the children laugh.

Bill, however, was a harder nut to crack.

After the kids had gone to bed, he pondered in silence over the washing up. The kitchen sink was always his thinking place and as he swished water over the cups and plates, I sensed he was weighing it all up.

"What do you reckon, love?" I asked gently as I picked up a tea-towel and started to dry the crockery. "Would we be biting off more than we can chew?"

"Possibly," he replied. "This Susan sounds like she could cause trouble. I can deal with the fall-out, but I'm worried about the effect she might have on the kids."

He was right, of course, and I agreed with every word.

"There again," he continued, "we knew from the start that fostering would never be an easy ride. What do you think we should do, Jeanie?"

I shook my head in uncertainty. Looking after a pregnant young girl presented one set of challenges I felt equipped to tackle, but trying to protect her from outside influences while moderating her lack of boundaries was uncharted territory for me.

"I guess it's what we signed up for, Bill," I said cautiously. "But if we're not ready for this, we don't have to do it. Carol will understand."

Bill sighed and scratched his head.

"Ok, let's give it a try," he said, placing the last washed plate on the draining board. "If Susan gets out of hand or upsets the kids, we'll ask Carol and Janet to step in.

"Susan's only a teenage girl, after all, and a pregnant one at that. How tricky can she be? She just needs a bit of stability around her, that's all. We can give her that."

I smiled at Bill's reassuring optimism. He had always had a knack of seeking out the best in people.

"You know what that means though, don't you, love?" I said, putting my arm around his shoulder. "You'll need to fetch that cot down from the loft again."

Just a Child

I've fostered young girls who would do anything for a drink or a cigarette. They felt so worthless that they'd even offer their bodies in return.

In their minds, any attention was better than no attention at all. Worst of all, they really believed that sex, no matter how cold and perfunctory, was real affection.

"Sex for some men is like going to the toilet, it's just a physical act," I'd warn them as they headed for the front door in a knicker-revealing skirt.

"There's no feeling in it for them, no emotion or commitment. He might finish with you tomorrow and how would you feel then?"

Some of the girls would roll their eyes like they knew it all and tell me I was being old-fashioned.

"If boys my age can do it, why can't I?" they'd ask. "What am I supposed to do? Save myself for my wedding day? Cos that ain't gonna happen!" And off they would go, slamming the door on their way out.

One of the girls I fostered celebrated her 16th birthday by having sex with the first boy she could lay her hands on.

"You don't have to do this, Sharon," I pleaded as she swanned out in a short skirt, high heels, low-cut top and a face full of make-up. "But I want to," she said, pouting childishly. "All my friends've dunnit. You can't stop me now. No-one can."

She was right about that.

"Why not wait a bit, meet someone you like first?"

My advice fell on deaf ears. In the mistaken idea that it would make her a proper grown-up, Sharon was determined to lose her virginity that night. She told me later that she'd had sex in an alleyway at the back of a pub with some spotty guy she had only just met.

"Well, I hope he wore a condom!" I said.

While young girls like her were physically ready to have sex, they were immature emotionally and never considered the consequences.

They would ignore my warnings, go out and sleep with guys they hardly knew, be on a high for five minutes, then come crashing down when they were subsequently ignored or tossed aside for the next willing girl.

As a result, these girls would feel even more worthless than they did before, but seek the attention of other men to bolster their self-esteem. And so the vicious circle continued.

Susan was already part of this damaging cycle when she came to us, eight months pregnant and with hardly any idea of how to look after herself, never mind a baby. She was, after all, still just a child herself, and a neglected one at that.

She'd had no family routine, no proper bedtime or mealtimes, so she had very little concept of how to behave in social situations, or as part of a family.

Having never received any parental care, she was used to fending for herself in a filthy flat, but she had hardly any idea how to perform many basic domestic tasks. She did somehow manage to keep her own bedroom fairly clean and tidy and also performed well at school, but trying to survive as a child in these dreadful conditions must have felt like a losing battle. When she stopped going to school and locked herself away in her room, her parents were too out of it to notice or care.

Then there was the company her parents would keep and bring into the house. Drug addicts, dealers and alcoholics would often crash out at the flat, and Susan became a target for all kinds of sickening attention from the sleazy men who congregated there.

It was only after one of them – or even her own father – gave her a black eye and bruises, that her hopeless situation was eventually discovered.

After being taken into care, all her suppressed anger and frustration erupted and she turned into a human volcano – volatile, unpredictable and capable of blowing up without warning.

She even changed her appearance. From being quite a mousy girl with non-descript, light brown hair who blended quietly into the background, she had transformed herself into a brassy, physically menacing delinquent.

So there were many reasons to be anxious about bringing Susan into our home and for wondering how we would all cope. And we didn't get off to the sunniest of starts.

As Carol drove me to meet her for the first time, she warned me that Susan could be "a bit intimidating, and not just in her manner." This would turn out to be something of an understatement.

When we parked in the gravel driveway of the children's home – an imposing but bleak Victorian house with ivy-covered walls – I saw a curtain twitch in one of the bedroom windows.

Looking up, I glimpsed a girl peering sullenly through the dusty pane, her dark eyes stark against her pale skin. For a moment I was startled by the penetrating stare and gloomy expression boring into me, and I shivered uneasily.

"Is that Susan standing in the window up there?" I whispered to Carol, quickly averting my gaze.

"Yes, that's her," she confirmed, glancing up. "She's expecting us. Don't let her manner put you off, though, Jeanie. If she knows she's spooked you out, she'll try it on even more."

I smiled wryly and nodded.

"Yes, I'll try to see through all the drama," I said, reminding myself that behind Susan's hostile appearance was a frightened, pregnant young girl who needed my help.

No sooner had Carol pulled the old-fashioned bell in the porch than one of the home's care workers opened the heavy front door and welcomed us in.

"Come through into the lounge," she said warmly, leading us into a spacious but rather drab communal room where Janet the social worker was already waiting for us.

"Hello Carol, Jeanie," she said tersely, glancing pointedly at her watch. "We're running five minutes late so we'd better get on with it."

It never ceased to amaze me how blunt Janet could be, but Carol was used to it.

"Sorry, Janet," she said breezily, sitting in an armchair and rummaging in her briefcase for her case notes.

"Right, I'll go and fetch Susan," declared Janet, marching briskly into the hallway and up the stairs.

I perched on a chair, glancing around at the large high-ceilinged sitting room. Decorated in fusty shades of green and grey, it was furnished with mis-matched sofas and the kind of chairs you find in a hospital waiting room. You could describe the overall style as "Sad, Wet Afternoon in an Institution".

It was adequate, but could have done with some comforting warmth and cosiness.

"What it needs is a splash of sunshine yellow," I imagined Bill, a painter and decorator, remarking. "Yellow always cheers you up, even on a rainy day."

Even so, this clinical grey room was probably a huge improvement on the filthy, cluttered flat where Susan had been brought up.

And there were signs of life here. The chairs clustered around the small black and white TV in the corner was where Susan would, I imagined, sit with the other girls to watch *Top of the Pops* and *Doctor Who* I somehow doubted that she was a *Blue Peter* fan.

Scattered around the swirly carpet were boxes of Monopoly and Ludo, and on the little tables dotted randomly around the room were abandoned games of cards, chess and draughts.

It reminded me of our lounge at home and I smiled as I remembered how my own kids still enjoyed playing these games.

I hoped that Susan would join them.

Suddenly, I heard heavy footsteps on the sweeping staircase in the hallway and muffled voices.

"I don't want-oo!" complained a girl's voice, followed by the loud stamp of a foot on the wooden floor. "Geddoffmee, you old cow!"

Staggering into the room with a frazzled Janet by her side, Susan then stood stock-still in the doorway. Her arms were folded defensively across her prominent bump as she stared at us with an expression of defiance. She was not, her body language said, coming any closer.

A tall girl with long, brassy bleached hair and dark roots, she had a face underneath all that make-up that I guessed would be very pretty if only it wasn't stuck in such a permanently sulky expression.

Dressed in a tight-fitting, long black dress that clung to her prominent baby bump, teamed with fishnet tights and spiky lace-up boots, it was a gothic look that had been carefully curated to match her mood.

She loomed, silent and glowering, over us all.

"Susan, this is Jeanie," said Janet, introducing us in slow, measured tones, as if she was speaking to someone with limited understanding. "This is the foster lady we told you about, the one you'll be living with for a bit."

Susan stared at her vacantly, her lip half curling into a sneer.

"Who?" she replied rudely.

It was clear to me that she wanted to wind up Janet, to punish her for looking down on her.

"You know full well what I'm talking about, Susan," replied Janet impatiently. "We talked about this yesterday. Jeanie's your new foster carer and she can help you with the baby."

With a friendly smile that I hoped would put this troubled girl at ease, I stood up and walked towards her.

"Nice to meet you, Susan," I said.

Ignoring my efforts at a polite introduction, she stared at me without blinking.

"I'm not going with her," she barked at Janet, nodding her head in my direction. "She looks like a right bitch."

I flinched and Carol looked horrified.

"That's quite enough of your language, young lady," rebuked Jane. "Jeanie's a very nice person and so is her family."

Susan's cheeks turned crimson, but I wasn't entirely sure whether it was from anger or embarrassment.

"As you are fully aware, this is the right thing for you and your baby," Janet continued, while Susan stared at the floor. "You'll be well looked after and you might make some nice friends for a change, too. One of Jeanie's daughters is about the same age as you."

Susan's interest seemed to prick up at the mention of Sarah.

"How old is she then?" she asked grudgingly, looking straight at me.

"She'll be 15 soon," I replied. "So nearly the same age as you. She's not as tall as you, mind."

Susan grinned.

"We're making progress," I thought. "I've actually made this moody girl smile!"

But there was an edge in Susan's manner that made me feel as if we were all walking on eggshells.

"Will I get my own room?" she asked, looking sideways at Janet as if this was a deal-breaker in a negotiation.

She had been sharing a bedroom with two other girls at the home, and from what I'd gathered, there had been friction between the hormonal trio, which had ended in a few physical spats with kicking, punching and hair-pulling.

Susan, through sheer strength, size and uninhibited aggression, had apparently come out on top each time. No wonder none of those girls had turned up to see her off.

"Oh yes, love," I confirmed with a smile before Janet could respond. "You'll have a bedroom to yourself."

It was not a pre-requisite in those days to provide a foster child with their own room – it was considered perfectly acceptable to share – but in light of Susan's condition, Bill and I had decided it was best for everyone if she and her baby had their own room.

She eyed me with suspicion.

"We've decorated it especially for you," I added. "I've put up new curtains to match, too."

Susan grinned self-consciously and fidgeted when I mentioned her freshly painted room. I don't suppose anyone had ever done anything like that for her and she seemed unsure how to react.

"We've put a little cot in there as well, for after your baby's born."

Her smile swiftly transformed into a frown and the expression in her eyes turned to fear.

"I'm not keeping it," she sniffed. "I wannit adopted."

"That's up to you, Susan," I said reassuringly. "But whatever you decide, that baby has to come out first. Let's just see how you feel about it after it happens, shall we?"

The tension was broken by the squeak of trolley wheels as the care worker trundled in with tea, biscuits and soft drinks, and we all sat down. Even Susan, tired from standing on her feet with her pregnancy bump, slumped into an armchair a few feet away from us.

Susan gulped back a glass of orange squash and I noticed that her fingernails, painted with chipped black nail polish, were bitten down to the quick.

Wiping her mouth on her sleeve, she let out an enormous belch in our direction. Observing Janet's expression of disgust, Susan's eyes glinted mischievously.

"Manners, Susan," the care worker gently remonstrated. "We don't break wind in company."

"Don't *we*?" said Susan, glaring at her in contempt. "Well I *do*."

It was almost comical and to be expected, really, as Susan tested us with her rudeness.

I sensed a battle of wills ahead. Well, two could play at that game.

"Oh, don't worry about it," I said casually. "You should hear my kids. They're like wind machines! Sometimes they have competitions to see who can burp the loudest."

Janet immediately shot me a look of disapproval, while Carol suppressed a smile and the care worker looked away in embarrassment.

Meanwhile, Susan cackled like a drain. Her insulting behaviour had not provoked the reaction she had anticipated – and my remark seemed to appeal to her sense of humour.

"I think she's beginning to like me," I thought in relief.

Little did I know that Susan's belches would be the least of my problems.

"So who won the contest?" she asked earnestly. "I bet I can beat 'em all."

"Um, well," I stuttered, thrown by the fact that she had taken me at my word. "I think my little boy, Stevie, usually wins first prize."

It felt peculiar having a conversation with Susan about such a silly subject at our first meeting, and so I was relieved for once when Janet interjected, bringing us back to earth with a bump.

"This is getting very childish," she declared, draining her tea and purposefully clinking the cup neatly back on to the saucer. "We need to move on."

I suspected that her comment was partly aimed at me for encouraging Susan's juvenile shock tactics, but I had to gain ground with this girl somehow if we were going to wrench her from the place that had been her home for a year.

An emotionally damaged child, she would need all the help she could get – and I would need all the patience I could muster – to see her through to childbirth and beyond.

"So what do you think?" I overheard Janet ask Susan in the hallway when it was time for Carol and me to leave. "Do you like Jeanie?"

"She's alright," she sniffed. "Anyway, I bet her place is better than this dump!"

High praise indeed.

But were Bill and I – and the kids – ready to welcome this stroppy teenage girl into our home?

"She's got a bit of a temper on her," I warned them over our fish and chip supper later. "Mind you, I'd be angry, too, if I'd been through what she has."

Stevie and the girls giggled when they heard me mention how she'd belched in front of the adults.

"Can we have a contest?" Stevie asked hopefully.

"Absolutely not, young man," grinned Bill, tickling Stevie under the chin. "We're hoping, kids, that your good manners rub off on Susan, right?"

They nodded enthusiastically: at this point none of us could have imagined just how challenging our new house guest would turn out to be.

A few days later, after the foster placement had been officially confirmed, Carol and I returned to the home to pick up Susan.

With a baleful expression, she slowly trudged into the hallway to meet us.

"Are you packed and ready to go?" asked Janet, who had arrived shortly before us.

Susan nodded glumly.

"Right, I'll go and get your case. Fetch your coat, Susan; it's time to go."

As Janet sprang up from her chair, she quickly turned to the home's care worker.

"I almost forgot," she began, "when I was here yesterday I put some paperwork on the table in the kitchen. I noticed later that there were a few pages missing. Perhaps they slipped on to the floor. Has anyone found them, by any chance?"

The care worker looked blank, but Susan's smirk didn't escape me.

"You must be exhausted, love," I said, nodding at her bump. "I remember how tired I felt when I was ready to pop with my three."

Susan didn't react, preferring to pick off what remained of her black nail polish and brush it on to the floor.

"After tea tonight we'll get you settled in your room and you can have a good night's sleep," I said, only to be met with a resounding silence.

"It's a big change for you, Susan, but don't worry," I continued. "I'm going to look after you and make sure everything goes well with you – and the baby."

As I reached out to put my hand on her shoulder, she shrugged it off.

"I'm fine!" she snapped, staring morosely at the floor. "I don't want no pity."

Carol gave me a sympathetic wink and began to fold her papers into her briefcase. It seemed pointless to persist with Susan while she was in this antagonistic mood so we all waited, listening to the steady tick of the clock on the mantelpiece until Janet returned.

"All set?" she asked brusquely, her frame standing stiffly in the doorway as she gripped the handle of Susan's battered brown suitcase.

A pang of pity swept over me. The contents of that little bag – and the baby she was due to give birth to – were the only things this lost young girl had in the world.

She rose slowly to her feet and sauntered reluctantly towards the hallway.

"Stop dawdling," admonished Janet. To my surprise, Susan did as she was told.

"These young girls can be very stroppy," Janet said, having taken me quietly to one side. "We don't tolerate any rude or bad behaviour – and neither should you. Let me know immediately if she gives you any trouble."

With that prickly warning she was off and, without further delay, the care worker handed Susan a nondescript jacket from the coat-stand.

"Good luck," she said softly as Susan put it on. "Be good, won't you? And don't forget your manners with Jeanie and her family."

"Oh, and good luck with the baby," she added as an afterthought as we crunched across the gravel towards Carol's car.

The care worker's words were perfunctory and vaguely insincere, but not surprising, considering the stunts and shenanigans this troublesome teen had no doubt pulled while in her care.

Looking as if she was about to burst into tears, Susan stopped and looked back over her shoulder.

She had the face of an anxious child, hoping for reassurance from the only person who had even vaguely resembled a parent substitute since she'd lived in the home.

But it was too late. Her care worker was evidently so keen to get rid of her that she had already slammed the front door shut.

Susan looked crestfallen, but then her expression and entire attitude hardened as she shut away her disappointment.

Despite her unkind comments earlier, I felt a pang of compassion. I wondered how many times someone had shut the door on this troubled girl.

"Come on, love," I encouraged, holding opening the rear passenger door of Carol's car. "Let's get you comfy in the back."

Susan hesitated. She seemed to be looking around for someone, her head turning this way and that as if she expected this mysterious person to appear from behind the giant green fir tree in the unkempt garden.

"Have you forgotten something?" I asked, following her gaze.

"Nope," she said quickly, shaking her head. "I'm not looking for no-one."

With that telling response giving her away, and after one last dejected glance around her, she shuffled into the back seat.

"Let's get you strapped in," I said, stretching the seatbelt over her bump.

Susan wriggled awkwardly and as my hand inadvertently brushed against her arm, she pushed me away roughly.

"Geddoff!" she growled.

"Only trying to help you, Susan," I said, taken by surprise at her reaction and the force of her tone.

As I settled into the front seat, I could sense her stare boring into the back of my head. Glancing quickly around, my eyes locked with hers. She shot me a hostile scowl before looking away and staring aimlessly out of the window.

But in the blink of an eye, her expression switched from anger to sadness, and her eyes filled with tears.

"Are you ok, love?" I asked.

"Yeah!" she snapped, frantically wiping her hand across her face to hide her emotion. "Stop looking at me."

Carol shot me a look of dismay and I shrugged in confusion. I would have to keep reminding myself not to take anything too personally. I could only assume that she wasn't prepared to trust anyone in case they let her down.

As Carol backed her car out of the driveway into the tree-lined street, we saw a solitary figure lurking outside – presumably the person Susan had been desperately searching for.

A lanky young man in tight faded jeans and a grubby grey t-shirt was leaning against a lamppost, watching us with a defiant stare.

Puffing on a roll-up hanging out of the corner of his mouth, he flicked his dirty-blond hair off his pallid face.

I swivelled around to glance at Susan. Her face was animated now and she was smiling.

She unclipped her seatbelt excitedly and began to wind down her window.

"Mark!" she called through the gap, waving frantically at him. "I'm in here!"

Any minute now, I thought, she's going to open the door and jump out of the moving car.

"Susan, what are you doing?" I exclaimed. "Who's that boy?"

Sensing the urgency, Carol responded swiftly and stopped the car.

"You need to put your seatbelt back on, Susan," she ordered. "I can't drive us anywhere until you do."

Ignoring us both, Susan pulled a screwed-up piece of paper from the pocket of her dress and started to wave it through the open window.

Before we had time to react, the scruffy-looking lad had sprinted to the car and grabbed the crumpled sheet from her outstretched hand.

"Ta," he said gruffly. "Don't worry, I'll find yer."

It sounded more like a threat than a promise. Carol and I watched open-mouthed as he sauntered away with the scrunched-up piece of paper in his tobacco-stained hand and I somehow knew that we hadn't seen the last of him.

"Who's that boy, Susan?" I asked, trying not to betray in my voice my deep concern. "And what was that you gave to him?"

"It's Mark," she replied. "He's my boyfriend."

Then, with deliberate dramatic effect, she smugly added, "I was just giving him my new address."

Carol and I looked at each other in shock. Susan would not have been told yet where her foster family lived; the only person with that information was Janet from social services.

"So how do you know Jeanie's address?" asked Carol.

Susan gave a derisory snort.

"Dunno," she taunted. "I must 'ave seen it written down somewhere."

Then the penny dropped. That's where Janet's missing paperwork had gone. Susan was certainly devious enough to rummage through it when no-one was looking.

I shook my head in disbelief at her audacity.

We had barely left the children's home, yet already she had jeopardised the safety of us all and made us targets of harassment for Mark and his mob.

"Susan," said Carol crossly. "I hope you haven't invited Mark to Jeanie's house? He and his friends will certainly not be allowed to go there."

"But it's my home too, now," Susan replied insolently. "Aren't I allowed to have friends or nothing?"

"You aren't even living there yet," Carol reminded her. "And you have to ask permission to have visitors – just like at the home."

Abruptly slamming her car into gear, Carol sped off down the road, and the next ten minutes of the journey were spent in silence.

Glancing at Susan in the mirror, I could see that she was staring happily out of the window now.

From the smile on her face, it was obvious she was pleased that she had seen this lad – and was revelling in the agitation that handing him my address had caused.

"I'm so sorry, Jeanie," whispered Carol.

"Don't worry," I reassured her. "I had wondered if something like this might happen. That boy clearly has such a hold over her that she was bound to find a way to contact him. It just occurred sooner than I expected."

But inside I felt rattled and rather spooked by the idea of Mark and his pals turning up at our house.

"I'll file a report and talk to Janet straight away about a strategy," said Carol. "Rest assured, we'll give you all the support you need."

Bill and I would certainly need a procedure in place to shield our family – and Susan – should such a situation occur. Although I had a very strong feeling that, when it came to the crunch, our visitor would work against us and side with Mark.

As we turned the corner into my street, my mind was buzzing.

We climbed out of the car and walked around to the boot to retrieve Susan's case. "One thing has now become clear, though," I said quietly to Carol. "This is the first time she's admitted she's having a relationship with him and specifically named him. So I think there's a strong possibility he's the father of her baby."

Carol nodded in agreement.

If Mark already knew that Susan was pregnant with his baby, would it give him even more of a vice-like hold over her?

Before I could consider such a scenario I had to focus on my next priority – to introduce Susan to Bill and the kids.

Despite what had just occurred and my feeling of foreboding about the consequences, I wanted to get through our first meal together without some dramatic fall-out, and to help Susan settle in.

Susan eventually got out of the car and looked critically up and down the road at the houses around her. After waving Carol off, I picked up her case and gently ushered her towards the front door.

A New Home

As I put the key in the lock, a familiar sight made me smile. Through the glass in the front door I could see Sarah, Sophie and Stevie bundling into the hallway. They jostled excitedly for position, waving a hand-made card featuring a picture of us all on the front to welcome our newcomer.

I only hoped that Susan would appreciate the gesture and be friendly in return.

"Hello, Susan," Sarah said shyly, before Sophie echoed her words and Stevie piped up even louder.

If Susan's manner had been surly at the children's home, it was about to become positively obnoxious the moment she crossed our threshold.

My trio's warm greeting was met with what seemed like an icy indifference I found hard to fathom. Silent and stony-faced, Susan scanned each of them up and down with a dismissive cursory glance before looking away.

The children were confused and unsure how to react to this rude rejection.

Suddenly, Susan looked at the picture on her card then back at the kids, and spoke.

"'Ow come you look different to them two?" she asked Sarah. "You're white and they're brown."

I was mortified. Surely she wouldn't start talking about race the moment she'd arrived?

Momentarily stunned, the kids gawped at her as if they had no idea what she was talking about. It was only their similarities, not their differences, that they saw in one another.

But then Sarah spoke.

"Well, we have the same mum," she explained, "but different dads. A white one and a brown one.

"I've never seen my father, though," she added breezily. "Bill's my dad."

"Oooh, I see," Susan replied matter-of-factly, before adding with a grin, "I don't see my dad neither. And guess what colour his skin is?" she continued, with a crazy cackle. "Red and green!"

Stevie's eyes lit up.

"An alien?" he gasped.

"Yeah," teased Susan. "He's an alien all right. On another planet. He's red from being drunk all the time, and covered in green tattoos all over 'is body."

The girls looked horrified, but Stevie burst out laughing.

"Wow!" he said. "Green like Yoda in *Star Wars*!"

"Yeah, but he's evil like Darth Vader," she quipped.

Stevie giggled, but the girls looked at each other in confusion, unsure whether they should find any of what Susan had just told them funny, too.

The idea of describing someone's dad as "evil" really was alien to them.

"Where's my room, then?" demanded Susan. She cast her eyes over our small but cosy home with what appeared to be a sneer.

But after seeing the sterile, grey environment of the children's home and hearing a description of the sordid flat where she grew up – I realised that her look of disdain was a mask she put on when she felt overwhelmed.

"First things first, Susan," I said. "Let's take our coats off and then we'll carry your case up. You can freshen up and then we'll all eat our tea together, okay?"

"Yeah," she shrugged, as if she was doing me a favour.

Her mood had suddenly and inexplicably changed. Within the space of a minute she had switched from cracking jokes with the kids to studied indifference and hostility.

"I'm not sharing with her," she said, staring at Sarah.

"I've already told you, Susan, you have your own room," I reminded her.

"Probably best I don't share with no-one," she said. "I snore, so you won't get no sleep, not with all that racket. And with this baby pressing down on me bladder, I need the bog a lot in the night."

Stevie and Sophie smirked in amusement and embarrassment, while Sarah pursed her lips in indignation. She hadn't forgiven Susan for singling her out – nor did she like her vulgar remarks about the toilet.

Susan was certainly not the sort of girl Sarah would ever have as a friend – usually the sort of girl who liked pretty colours, dressing up games and playing beauty salons.

They were polar opposites, and although our newcomer was too tough to let it show, each made the other one feel small.

Observing Sarah's delicate nature and sensitivity, Susan had set out to dominate and shock.

"I'm bustin' for a wee again," she said, wriggling from foot to foot. "Where's the bog?"

"Just over there," I said, pointing to door under the stairs. "That's our downstairs *toilet*."

Although Stevie and Sophie were still grinning in bemusement at Susan's unusual manner, Sarah was fuming.

"Mam, she's so rude," she whispered. "I don't like it."

I stroked Sarah's hair reassuringly. "Let's give her a chance, love. She's only just got here."

Sarah nodded and wandered back to the safety of the kitchen where Bill was preparing our tea.

Although I cringed at the way Susan was speaking and behaving, I decided not to reprimand her so soon after she had arrived. I would, however, need to tackle her behaviour before too long.

"Right, let me take your case upstairs for you," I said brightly after she emerged from the toilet.

But as I lifted it up, I heard the sound of glass clinking against glass.

Susan looked startled.

"That's me make-up bottles," she babbled, leaping forward with lightning speed to grab the case out of my hand. "Careful, you'll break 'em. I'll do it meself, ta." As she attempted to lug the heavy bag to the bottom step, Bill suddenly appeared in the hallway.

"Welcome to our crazy home, Susan," he quipped, his trademark sunny smile instantly lighting up the room.

"Hello... Bill," she simpered, looking up at him through her mascara-caked eyelashes.

It was extraordinary to watch how her attitude and body language changed in the presence of a man. Switching from defensive and hostile to manipulative minx, she turned to face him.

It was blatantly flirtatious behaviour.

Bill looked embarrassed and cleared his throat.

"I'll carry that for you, love," he said, taking the case from her hand. "We can't have pregnant ladies lifting heavy objects now, can we?"

Susan looked surprised and her face flushed beneath her chalky foundation. Bill's chivalry, it seemed, was a quality she had never experienced before in a man.

"Cheers, chuck," she said, licking her red lips and flashing him a smile.

"All part of the service, ma'am," he replied chirpily as he bounded upstairs to deposit the suitcase in her room.

Standing in the hallway, Susan stared after him, brazenly ogling his muscular form.

The glint in her eye, and the inappropriate way she behaved right in front of me, as if I was invisible, made me feel uneasy. But this girl's boundaries, I reminded myself, had been eroded by the adults around her from a very early age.

She really had no idea how to behave and really it wasn't her fault.

"Come on, Susan," I said matter-of-factly, showing her upstairs. "The bathroom's over there and this is your room."

I opened the door to the bedroom Bill had recently painted.

I'd finished it off with a lovely new primrose candlewick bedspread and matching yellow curtains.

"Yeah, it'll do," she said ungraciously, which wasn't quite the reaction I had hoped for after all our hard work.

But despite her lukewarm response, I could tell from the way her eyes sparkled as she scanned the bright, fresh décor that she secretly liked it.

Bill had thoughtfully placed her suitcase on her bed, so that she didn't have to bend over to lug it off the floor. After clicking it open, Susan began to unpack her clothes, most of which seemed to be in 50 shades of black and very revealing: two mini skirts, an assortment of virtually transparent mesh tops, a low-cut tight dress identical to the one she was wearing, skimpy black knickers and lacy bras, and a tangled nest of fishnet tights.

It seemed the only item that wasn't black was a pale-blue baby doll nightie, which seemed out of place in that sea of darkness.

"Can I help you, love?" I asked as she began to shove the garments in a higgledy-piggledy mass inside the chest of drawers. "Here, let me fold them for you."

Susan leapt defensively between me and her case.

"No!" she barked, her glance darting back and forth between me and a dome-shaped mound inside her luggage. "I'm doing it."

I was startled by her vehement response. She was evidently trying to hide something.

Was it the glass that I heard clinking earlier? She'd claimed it was her make-up bottles that had made the noise.

"Sorry love, shall I just take your toiletries to the bathroom then?" I asked her.

"Yeah, all right, go on," she said, handing me her sponge bag. "I'm keeping me perfumes in me room, though."

Perhaps it was the scent bottles I'd heard chinking together? Or was it something less innocent? I tried hard not to make assumptions.

There was nothing made of glass among her toiletries: just a toothbrush, a small tube of toothpaste, a flannel and, I noted with a smile, a peach soap on a rope just like the ones we'd bought for Sarah and Sophie at Christmas.

Bill and the kids were already in the kitchen waiting for us. With perfect timing as we walked in, Bill was dishing up his famous jerk chicken with rice, while Sarah, Sophie and Stevie were in their usual places at the table, fiddling with their cutlery and snatching nervous, uncertain looks at the bleached blonde newcomer.

They had only ever seen girls wearing so much make-up singing in bands on the telly – or loitering in groups, smoking cigarettes and drinking cider down the park.

"Are you a punk rocker?" blurted Stevie, intrigued and a little overawed by Susan's striking appearance.

"Don't be silly, Stevie," tutted Sophie. "She looks more like Debbie Harry from Blondie than a punk girl."

While Sarah sat in silence, glancing suspiciously at our larger-than-life guest, Susan beamed.

"Yeah, a lot of people tell me I look like Debbie," she said proudly, running a hand through her brittle blonde hair.

"Really?" asked Sarah in disbelief, to which Susan shot her an angry look.

It was time for me to step in.

"Here you go, love," I beckoned to our guest and pulled out a chair for Susan next to Sarah. "You two are the eldest so you can be neighbours at the table."

I thought this would make Susan feel special and unite the two girls, whose introduction had got off to a rocky start. But it seemed to have the reverse effect.

"Nah," grimaced Susan, plonking herself down at the opposite end of the table, right next to Bill. "I'm all right here."

Sarah's cheeks flushed in humiliation. This was the second time Susan had rejected Sarah and she looked as if she was going to cry.

I put a comforting hand on Sarah's shoulder as I placed her tea on the tablemat in front of her, trying to conceal my disquiet at our guest's unprovoked spite.

I knew there would inevitably be ructions with Susan at some point, but I hadn't anticipated that they would begin quite so soon. Instead of bonding over their closeness in age, a power struggle between the two girls had ensued, and it was down to me to diffuse the situation.

Pretending to ignore Susan's unkindness, I began to dish out the jerk chicken – specially made from a recipe handed down through the generations in Bill's family – while Sarah filled everyone's glasses with orange squash.

But when she reached over to pour it into Susan's glass, Susan slammed her hand across the top.

"Don't like orange squash," she said bluntly, as Sarah stood there poised with the jug, confused about what to do next. "I want lemonade."

This was Susan's childish attempt at riling Sarah by being difficult. Only an hour earlier, she had been gulping back orange squash at the children's home.

Yet like many troubled youngsters from broken backgrounds, she was being deliberately provocative to get the attention she had lacked as she was growing up, venting her anger on the innocent people around her.

"We only have orange squash or water, Susan," I said calmly. "Which would you prefer?"

Wrinkling her nose at the mention of water, she lifted her glass for Sarah to fill it with orange.

"Go on then, Sarah," she ordered. "Fill her up."

Just as she had done at the home, Susan gulped it back then wiped her mouth on her sleeve, smudging her lipstick across her face in the process.

Then came her revolting party trick. She punctuated the movement with a sequence of loud belches, looking around the table as if to say, "What do you think of that, then?"

Although Sophie giggled, her big sister was not amused. Still smarting from Susan's unfriendly treatment of her, Sarah looked down at her plate with an expression of disgust.

Stevie, however, was shaking with laughter.

"I can do that too!" he said, drinking a mouthful of squash in preparation.

But as he and Susan geared up to entertain us with another round of belching, Bill raised his eyebrows and I shook my head in disapproval.

"Please don't do that while we're eating," I said firmly, looking first directly at the ringleader and then at Stevie, who proceeded to swallow his squash.

"That goes for everyone," I stressed. "If you feel the need to do that sort of thing, you should go to the bathroom, please. Remember, manners at mealtimes."

In the space of only an hour of her arrival, Susan had managed to dominate, disrupt and divide, albeit in a childlike way.

She stared at me with a defiant smile. She had lost respect for herself and therefore, it seemed, she had none for us either.

Clearing his throat, Bill tried to distract the kids from our young guest's juvenile behaviour by focusing on the meal.

"For those who clear their plates, we have apple crumble and custard for afters," he said with a wink, to three cries of appreciation.

Susan, however, was sullenly pushing her rice and chicken around her plate. When she finally lifted a small morsel of chicken to her lips, she stared at it as if it had come from another planet.

"Too spicy for you?" asked Bill casually.

Susan churlishly pushed her plate away.

"Yeah, I'm not used to this foreign muck," she said. "The chicken's got stuff on it and tastes funny."

I bristled, bracing myself in case she went on to insult Bill's West Indian heritage as well as his cooking.

If Bill was offended, he didn't show it.

"Just eat what you can and I'll remember to make yours a bit milder next time," he said calmly.

Susan's ungracious response not only showed her ignorance, it also revealed the lack of variety in her unhealthy diet.

"So what food do you like, Susan?" he asked. "Once we know your favourites, we can start making them for you."

"Dunno," she replied flatly. "Chocolate and burgers mainly. And crisps. I like getting takeaways from the chippy, too."

The kids stared at her in bemusement as she listed the things they would only ever have been allowed to eat as treats, not main courses at mealtimes.

"I've never had rice before, though," she continued, spooning it up then letting it fall back onto her plate. "And I hate veg."

No wonder she looked so pale, I thought. She's not getting her vitamins.

"Perhaps you'd like to do some cooking with me one day?" I suggested. "Then you can learn how to prepare meals and I'll show you how to make fresh baby food for your little one."

Susan wrinkled her nose and shook her head.

"Nah," she said. "I've not got time for all that rubbish. And I won't be feeding this baby nothing, I'm 'avin it adopted."

A shocked silence followed and a gloomy atmosphere descended.

It's your fault, Jeanie, I thought to myself. I had spoken too soon about the baby, especially as Susan still hadn't properly considered her options.

Bill distracted us all by changing the subject.

"Who wants crumble?" he called out, with a wink to me.

Our three kids cheered, while Susan clattered her knife and fork dismissively on to her plate.

As we all tucked into Bill's apple crumble, she sat back in her chair with her hand on her bump, staring at us one by one. The only part of the pudding she would deign to eat was the custard.

"Homework now, kids," Bill said breezily, getting up from the table to clear the plates. "Then it's bath and bed."

As our three youngsters charged upstairs, Susan sat alone at the table in peevish silence. She was a handful alright, but she was also a pregnant teenager who hadn't been taught how to give and receive love.

Susan's behaviour – lashing out to conceal her fear of the unknown – was understandable and expected. Not that this made it easy to deal with. But I knew I had to see beyond the surface if I was to stand any chance of reaching out to her.

There was a lot less sympathy for girls like her in those days, especially if, like Susan, they looked older than they actually were.

Nobody seemed to realise that there was a vulnerable child behind the tough façade, a victim who needed protection, not punishment.

That's why, in spite of the upset Susan deliberately caused when she first arrived at our home, it would have been unfair to blame her completely for her lack of manners, her cruel remarks and her anti-social behaviour.

I certainly planned to attempt to smooth away her jagged edges, though, and reach the lonely, frightened girl inside.

When Bill and I had finished clearing away and doing the washing up, I turned around to speak to her.

She leaned back and let out an enormous, loud yawn.

"You must be exhausted," I said, mindful that in this late stage of her pregnancy she would need plenty of rest. She would also need far more nourishment than she had consumed for her tea.

"Shall I make you a hot milky drink to take up to bed with you, Susan?" I asked.

She looked at me with a flicker of gratitude, then gazed blankly at the floor and nodded.

Was she ashamed of her performance at the table that evening – or simply annoyed at having to eat unfamiliar food with a group of strangers?

It can't have been easy for her, suddenly being installed with a family she didn't know.

But acting up, I realised, was her way of asserting herself, of making herself feel that she actually mattered. What did she care if she was getting attention for all the wrong reasons? It was still attention.

Then, when the focus was no longer on her, she became despondent and withdrawn.

"If there's anything you need, Susan, just ask me," I said kindly as I handed her a hot cup of cocoa and a plate of biscuits. "This is your home now, remember. Treat it as your own."

As she shuffled off to bed, I turned to Bill.

"What do you make of our newcomer, then?" I whispered.

Wiping his hands on a tea towel, he raised his eyebrows and grinned.

"What's with all that belching business? It took us ages to get the kids out of that silly habit. I hope they don't think they can start it up again. We'll have to crack down on it, especially when my mum comes over for tea on Sunday. She'll have a fit!"

Imagining Ivy's shocked indignation made us both burst into fits of giggles.

Although we knew that Susan's poor table manners were the least of our worries, it felt good to share a laugh: we needed the light relief after such an emotionally draining evening.

Laughter kept us sane. Without being flippant about any situation we encountered as foster carers, we found that a sense of humour got us through most of the challenges that came our way.

Persuading Susan to toe the line would be a battle of wills, but at least after her first evening in our home, we understood what we were dealing with.

And no matter what we faced ahead with Susan, my own children's wellbeing and happiness was my priority. Before bedtime, I went up to check on them.

When I peered around the door into Stevie's room, he was already in bed and about to fall asleep. Stroking his forehead, I gave him a kiss goodnight before tip-toeing to his sisters' room next door.

Sophie was dozing off on the bottom bunk, but Sarah was sitting bolt upright on the top deck, her purple bedspread pulled tightly around her.

She looked pale and forlorn.

"What's wrong, love?" I asked, putting a comforting arm around her.

She shrugged her shoulders and glanced away.

"It's Susan, isn't it?" I continued. "She's upset you."

Sarah nodded.

"Why doesn't she like me, Mum? I've tried being nice to her, but she seems to hate me. She wouldn't even sit next to me at the table."

It pained me to see my eldest daughter distressed by a person I had brought into our home.

But I had to remind myself that we always knew fostering would involve looking after damaged children who would lash out and probably cause mayhem.

It was my role to smooth over the tensions, to try to maintain cordial relationships between the newcomer and my family and, above all and no matter how difficult it seemed, to treat that child as if she or he was one of my own.

"Try not to take it to heart," I advised Sarah, giving her a hug. "Susan's unkindness isn't directed at you, really – she's angry with the entire world because of what's happened to her."

"So why was she nastiest of all to me when she got here?" she asked with a puzzled frown. "I've tried being nice to her but… the way she looks at me is horrible, Mum. She's horrible."

Sarah was absolutely right, of course; Susan's treatment of her had been spiteful and unnecessary.

If it continued, there would be disciplinary consequences that would involve Janet, the social worker.

Until then, I would try my best to help Sarah under-stand that Susan's motives were not personal but stemmed from her feelings of anger and sadness towards the people who were meant to care for her.

"The thing is, Sarah," I began, "unlike you, Susan's had a very difficult life so far. You're the age she was when she got pregnant. So when she looks at you, she probably sees the girl she wishes she could have been – one who's loved and cared for, with a nice home and family.

"Your life is opening up, you'll grow up and enjoy your freedom. When she looks at her life, though, I'll bet it seems to be shutting down. She's got no family apart from us, a group of strangers, and on top of everything, she knows that she has to give birth in a few weeks' time. She's only a little bit older than you."

She listened intently, mulling over what our young guest had been through and imagining how she felt.

"OK," she whispered eventually. "She must be very frightened. I'll try to help her if I can, Mum."

Then she summed up the situation with the wisest words of all.

"Susan is mean to everyone because she's hurting," she said, "but Angela kept her hurt inside."

"That's right, love," I agreed. "Until we walk in their shoes, we have no idea how we would react, whether we would be more like Susan or more like Angela."

It was a lot to process in one night, and with a yawn, Sarah curled up beneath her blankets and settled down.

"Will Susan be coming to school with me tomorrow?" she asked sleepily. "We could be in the same class."

I shook my head.

"I'm afraid not, love," I said. "It won't be long before Susan's baby is born and until then I'll be helping her to get ready for it. We have a lot to do."

Smoothing Sarah's blonde hair away from her face, I gave her a peck on the cheek. Her eyelids were heavy and as she closed them, I walked quietly to the door.

"Night, love," I whispered. "Sleep well."

As I wandered back across the landing, I could see a light shining through the narrow gap at the bottom of Susan's bedroom door. Was she still awake?

"Are you all right, Susan?" I called softly.

When there was no response, I opened the door a chink to peer inside.

Sprawled out across the bed, still in her black dress, fishnets and boots, Susan was sound asleep.

Her face betrayed no sign of the aggression or attitude we'd witnessed from her earlier: she was just a vulnerable young girl who looked as if she'd gone overboard with her mum's make-up. A pregnant young girl who'd already seen and experienced more than any teenager should have done, and who was about to face her biggest challenge yet.

Stepping gingerly into the room, I placed a blanket over her and switched off her bedside lamp before heading back downstairs to find Bill.

He was whistling away contentedly in the kitchen, making the kids' packed lunches for school the next day alongside his own. I was about to cast a cloud over his sunny sandwich making: I knew this was my moment to tell him about the incident with Mark outside the children's home.

"We may have a problem, love," I began, watching him arrange slices of cheese, lettuce and tomato on to the buttered bread.

"Yep, she's a tricky one, all right, Jeanie," he replied, placing the foil-wrapped sandwiches into lunchboxes. "Nothing we can't handle, though."

"No, there's something else," I said. "Someone else."

Bill stopped what he was doing and looked at me intently.

"As we were leaving the home, Susan managed to hand that boy – Mark – our address," I explained. "I think she stole the paperwork from Janet."

A shadow fell over Bill's face as he realised that we – but more importantly, the kids – could now be sitting targets.

"Does he have a criminal record for violence?" he asked.

"I don't think so. From what I've been told, he's a bit of a rogue and a thief. There's drink and drugs involved with his gang, too, but only on a small scale.

"The worst of it for me is the way he's taken advantage of an underage girl. We think he's the one who got Susan pregnant when she was 14."

Placing the kids' lunchboxes on the kitchen table, Bill shook his head.

"Are we sure we're doing the right thing letting her stay here, Jeanie?" he frowned. "What if she lets that yob Mark in when we're out?"

I must admit, I had questioned the wisdom of allowing Susan to jeopardise our family's safety, too.

But to send her packing back to the children's home so early would seem like a defeatist move to me. And potentially very damaging for Susan.

"It's too soon to give up on her," I said. "Besides, we always knew this job was going to be tough at times. Let's give her a couple of weeks or so to settle in and calm down."

Bill nodded in agreement. Once he was onside, that was it.

"If Mark comes anywhere near her – or anyone else in this house – he'll have me to deal with," he said fiercely.

As with every youngster Bill and I fostered over the years, we would protect Susan as if she was our own daughter.

"When they're under our roof, they're one of us," Bill would always declare.

There were times, however, when it often felt as if we were the ones needing protecting – from our rebellious young guests.

After collapsing exhausted into bed that night, we had no idea what the following days would bring. But we did know that whatever happened around Susan would inevitably involve a heavy helping of drama.

Kicking Off

At 6am next morning Bill, the kids and I launched into our usual routine, otherwise known as organised mayhem.

It was always a mad flurry that began with the jarring metallic clatter of my alarm clock, followed by waking up the kids, making them breakfast while I was still half asleep, and the dizzying process of getting them ready for school – which could only be described as a bit like herding kittens.

I'd decided to let Susan sleep late on her first morning and assumed that she was still out for the count while our whirlwind of activity went on around her.

Eventually, however, the sound of feet scurrying up and down the stairs in search of lost pencil cases and cries of "Where's my blazer?" were loud enough to wake her.

Then, out of the corner of my eye as I stirred a saucepan of scrambled eggs, I caught a glimpse of her wafting into the kitchen.

When I glanced up to say "good morning", I did a double take.

Susan was wearing the blue baby-doll nightie and it barely covered her backside.

I could hardly bring myself to look.

"Mornin'." she said, sleepily stretching out her arms and yawning.

When she turned around, I could see that this nightie was practically transparent at the top. As she sat at the table and poured herself some juice, Bill and the kids got an eyeful.

Sarah stormed out in disgust, Sophie gawped at her in shock and Bill averted his gaze in embarrassment.

"Where's your dressing gown, Susan?" said Stevie, asking the question that was on all of our minds.

"What?" Susan growled, oblivious to the impact of her revealing attire.. "I haven't got one. Why?"

"You must be cold," I quickly interjected. "But I've got a spare dressing gown you can wear. Sophie, go and fetch it please. It's the pink one on the back of my bedroom door."

As Sophie raced upstairs, I took a deep breath.

"Right, Susan, would you like scrambled or fried?"

Judging by the expression of confusion on her face, she was genuinely flummoxed by the stir her night-dress had caused.

Walking around half naked was normal to her.

I gave a quiet sigh of relief when Sophie returned with the dressing gown and handed it to Susan.

"Ta," she said, flinging it on but leaving it undone at the front. "This chair's much warmer on my arse now."

I flinched at her crude language and constant tendency to draw attention to her body.

But once again I had to remind myself that not only had she been given no boundaries by adults, she had been exposed to a depraved atmosphere from an early age. Until she came to live with us, her only relationship with men had been sexual and she knew no other way of communicating with them.

In addition to the likelihood that she had been molested by the addicts who visited her home, Susan had gone on to be groomed as a teenager by Mark and his sleazy entourage.

She had learnt to view her body as a currency, a means to manipulate, seduce and generally get her own way.

It had become second nature to her, a grotesque habit of which she was hardly even aware.

"Pass the ketchup please, Bill," she said, flicking her blonde fringe out of her kohl-smudged eyes.

She squeezed the red sauce all over her scrambled egg, but as she began to mix it all up, looked at my husband and suggestively licked some of the ketchup that had splashed on to her fingers. It was a repulsive display.

Clearing his throat, Bill stood up abruptly and, pushing his chair noisily across the floor behind him, boomed, "Right, kids, time for school!"

Whether she was aware of it or not, Susan had put on a hideously provocative piece of theatre and it was time for me to nip it in the bud.

After everyone else had left, I poured two cups of tea from the pot and sat beside her.

"Susan, we need to have a serious chat," I said. "There are a few house rules you need to know about."

Rolling her eyes, she threw down her knife and fork. "Hang on a minute," she declared. "I need the bog."

Keeping a lid on my frustration, I cleared away the breakfast things and awaited her return. While it was to be expected at this advanced stage of her pregnancy that she would frequently need the toilet, she didn't come back to the kitchen for almost half an hour.

From the smell of tobacco on her breath, it was obvious what she had been doing in there.

"Right, Jeanie, what did you want to tell me?" she asked. "Have I done summat wrong?"

Oh, where to begin, I thought to myself.

"Well, Susan, first of all, it's fine to walk around in your nightdress in your own room, but when we are around other people, we need to make sure we're covered up."

She stared at me as if I was speaking a foreign language.

"Why?" she asked. "What's wrong with me nightie? It was me mum's."

I could see that I was going to have to spell it out.

"To be honest, you're showing off too much flesh," I explained. "Look Susan, it's just not right for you to be putting your bottom and boobs on display. Didn't anyone at the children's home ever talk to you about this?"

Susan shrugged.

"Dunno, we never listened to that care worker anyway," she said. "Look, I haven't got any other nightie, what do you want me to wear? How about nothing?" She threw her head back with a cackle.

Whatever problems Susan had, she also possessed a strong sense of humour, dark though it was.

"Look, I have some pyjamas and a nightie that will fit you," I said. "You're welcome to have them – as well as the dressing gown you're wearing."

Susan paused to consider, as if dressing properly in our home was a suggestion she could decline.

"Okay," she nodded slowly, evidently under the impression that she was doing me a favour and not the other way around. "Is that all, then?"

"No, Susan, there are a few more ground rules to discuss, I'm afraid," I said, taking a deep breath. "I can smell tobacco. I think you might have been smoking just now? We don't allow cigarettes in the house. It goes without saying, they're a fire hazard.

"And you're only 15 – you're not old enough to smoke and it's not good for you."

It seems strange nowadays that I would have to spell out the health hazards of smoking, but it was different back in the 70s. Although the dangers were known and printed on cigarette packets, smoking was a widespread habit and even kids could buy them at the corner shop as long as they claimed they were for an adult relative. Pregnant women and nursing mothers smoked, too, as the threat to the health of a mother and her baby was not recognised in the same way that it is now.

"I'll go for a puff outside in the garden then," said Susan.

"No, I'd prefer you not to buy cigarettes at all," I insisted.

Susan's cheeks flushed and she looked away.

"I don't buy 'em."

"What, so you steal them then?"

"No! A friend gives 'em to me."

It was obvious who she meant.

"That brings me to the next thing," I continued. "No visitors are allowed into the house without permission from me or Bill."

I was referring to Mark, of course, and she knew it.

"You gave our address to that young man outside the children's home," I said. "Neither he nor his friends are welcome here, Susan. It will be a matter for the police if he shows up on our doorstep, do you understand?"

"Yeah, okay Jeanie," she said, with a reluctant, unconvincing nod.

But as she was leaving the room, she looked over her shoulder and stuck two fingers up at me.

My heart sank. Laying down the law with this young lady was going to be a tricky task, with more ups and downs than a rollercoaster – only minus the thrills.

Later that morning Carol and Janet arrived for Susan's placement meeting.

She was stretched out on our sofa like the Queen of Sheba, flicking through the channels on our telly, when they walked in. So non-existent were her manners that she didn't even have the good grace to look up and say hello.

"Come on Susan, switch that contraption off!" snapped Janet, standing with her hands on her hips in front of the screen. "We need to talk."

With a long-suffering sigh – and smirking at Janet's peculiar description of the TV as a "contraption" – Susan switched off the TV and gave her a mock salute.

"Silly girl," huffed Janet, rummaging in her briefcase for her clipboard. "Now look, Susan, I'm going to ask you a serious question and I need an honest answer. Did you steal the paperwork containing Jeanie's address that I left on the table at the children's home?"

Susan's cheeks flushed and she wriggled nervously in her seat.

"No, I didn't *steal* it," she replied slyly.

Janet raised a quizzical eyebrow.

"I borrowed it, Janet," continued Susan. "I 'ad a right to know where I would be living."

Carol and I looked at each other and rolled our eyes. This kind of juvenile response was typical of youngsters like Susan. Since their lives had been blighted by a blurring of the lines, they knew how to use it to their advantage.

"I see, so you *borrowed* it," said Janet icily. "In that case, please can you fetch it from your room and return it to me now."

It was checkmate to Janet. Or was it?

After a brief pause, Susan calmly went upstairs and, a minute later, came back down with a sheet of folded paper.

"Here you go," she said triumphantly, handing it to Janet. "Your precious paperwork."

Sure enough, when Janet opened it up, she saw my address on the page, written in her handwriting: it was the original missing sheet.

We were flabbergasted: how did she still have the paper?

"So what did you hand to Mark through the window of my car, Susan?" asked Carol. "What was written on that piece of paper?"

Susan lowered her eyes.

"It was a letter," she muttered. "A love letter from me."

Just as I breathed a sigh of relief that she hadn't told Mark our whereabouts after all, she said, "And I copied down this address for him, too."

My heart sank.

This was a serious breach of security: Carol and Janet were livid. Looking Susan straight in the eye, Janet warned, "If that young man comes anywhere near this house, we will call the police immediately. *Do you understand?*"

Janet's angry voice had the power to strike fear into anyone who stepped out of line. Even I trembled slightly as I watched its effect on Susan, who was suddenly shaking like a leaf. But perhaps she was just afraid of what might happen to her "boyfriend".

"Yes, I understand," she murmured. "I don't want him to be arrested. Sorry."

Janet nodded. "Go to your room, Susan, and reflect on what you've done. You have a baby to prepare for now. And just to be sure we really do understand each other, I expect your behaviour to improve. Jeanie will file a written report to me about you every day. Off you go."

While Susan slunk away, the caution ringing in her ears, Carol, Janet and I discussed how to deal with this young tearaway.

With just a few weeks to go before she brought a new life into the world, we certainly had our work cut out.

"She needs to be watched closely, Jeanie," insisted Janet. "If Mark continues to exert such a dangerous influence on her – or turns up at the house – call us, and the police, immediately."

I nodded vigorously, wondering what I'd got us all into. It was all very well for me and Bill to try and do our bit to help others, but I didn't want to put my own children in any danger.

"Oh, and as for Susan's terrible manners, don't hesitate to call her out on them straight away," Janet added, as she left with Carol.

How did Janet know about her bad manners? I wondered. I hadn't mentioned those.

Noticing my surprised expression, she explained: "We all heard about the belching and wot-not at the children's home. She does it for attention."

I had worked that one out already. But how was I to deal with Susan's attention-seeking antics? Although I understood Janet's insistence on discipline, I reminded myself that Susan's dysfunctional behaviour was her defence mechanism.

In my parenting role, I felt that it was my job to break through it gently, not with a sledgehammer. As my mam used to say, "You catch more flies with honey than vinegar, Jeanie."

This was easier said than done with Susan, though.

After Janet and Carol's departure, she became uncharacteristically quiet and subdued. When the kids came home from school and tried to engage her in conversation, she replied in monosyllables, or with a nod and shake of her head.

Over tea, she seemed to be in a world of her own, barely eating or speaking, before retreating into her room as soon as she possibly could.

When I walked past her door to wish her and the kids goodnight, I could hear sobbing from inside.

"Susan, are you all right?" I called softly through the door.

There was a sniff followed by silence. She had decided not to communicate with me and I felt it best to give her some space to recover. It was hard to hear Susan sobbing her heart out and not be able to comfort her as I would my girls.

"Susan was very restrained tonight," remarked Bill as we tidied up downstairs.

"Yes, that Janet gave her a bit of an earful," I replied. "I think it shook her up a bit. She's only a kid really – we all seem to forget that."

Bill nodded and smiled.

"Her hormones must be raging, too," he said. "Remember what you were like when you were expecting Stevie?"

"How could I forget!" I grinned. "I must have been a monster to live with!"

Bill chuckled.

"Too right you were! You were like a fierce, ravenous lioness," he teased. "I had to put a piece of raw meat on a stick and wave it into the room before I dared come in!"

As he walked past, I playfully flicked him with a teatowel for his cheek.

"I do feel sorry for the poor girl though," he said quietly. "Not much older than our Sarah and about to become a mum."

I sighed and shook my head at the unfairness of Susan's predicament. "She was crying her eyes out in her room just now. She must feel so scared."

The next day Susan was due for an antenatal check-up, but when she didn't join us all for breakfast, I assumed she had overslept.

"I'll go and check on her after you've taken the kids to school," I told Bill as he bundled our rowdy youngsters into the car. "Maybe she's just shattered; it's been an emotional time for her – and us!"

After Bill and the kids had left, I poured a glass of orange juice and a bowl of cornflakes for our guest and laid them out on the dining table.

But when there was still no sign of her, I went upstairs and tapped on her bedroom door.

"Are you awake?" I said softly.

Silence. I knocked louder this time.

"Susan, we need to set off for the clinic. You need to get up."

A muffled croak followed by the chinking sound of bottles. Oh, surely not…

I opened the door gently and peered in.

Susan was in total disarray. Entangled in the sheets on the floor, she was still wearing the same black dress from the day before. Her brittle blonde hair was sticking up all over the place and her trademark red lipstick and black kohl were smudged across her face.

But her shambolic appearance was not simply due to a bad night's sleep. There were damp patches under the arms, her face was bathed in beads of sweat and she was groaning.

In a panic, I wondered if her contractions had come early.

"Are you all right, Susan?" I gabbled. "Have your waters broken?"

"What?" she snapped, shooting me a look of contempt. "What waters? No they haven't!"

As I stepped forward to help her up, I was hit by two familiar aromas. A fug of tell-tale smoke hung in the air, as well as the sweet, distinctive smell of cider.

Judging by Susan's woozy expression, she'd had a skinful.

So, just as I had suspected, the rattling sound I heard in her suitcase was made by bottles of booze, not make-up.

She was either suffering from a hangover, or still drunk from swigging back cider in her room the night before. No wonder she hadn't come down for breakfast.

"You really shouldn't be drinking, Susan," I remonstrated. "You know it's not good for you or the baby."

"Mind your own," she spluttered, wiping her mouth with the back of her hand as she struggled to stand up.

"Here, let me help you," I said, leaping forward.

As I tried to catch hold of her arm, my foot kicked against a small tin on the floor, knocking a pile of ash and cigarette butts across the carpet.

Ignoring the smelly mess, I used all my strength to pull her to her feet.

"Are you all right?" I asked.

She was swaying precariously, her dizziness and prominent baby bump making her look like an egg-shaped weeble.

"I'm f-f-fine," she stammered. "Leave me alone."

But she was too dazed to protest with much force.

Easing her back on to the bed, I unlaced her high-heeled pointy boots. Her ankles were abnormally puffy, a dangerous symptom of pre-eclampsia, so I lifted them higher, placing a pillow underneath her legs in an attempt to bring down the swelling.

"You've been smoking, too, Susan," I said, flinging open a window to waft away the stale air.

"Well tha's my business, innit," she said, slurring her words.

"Susan, it's my business too, now. We don't allow smoking in this house – I've told you that before – and certainly no underage drinking."

From beneath her drooping eyelids, Susan stared at me vacantly, then closed her eyes.

"Yeah?" she shrugged dediantly. "So wotter you gonna do about it then?"

She was pushing all my buttons, but I managed to keep my voice calm.

"You're treading on very dangerous ground, Susan. It's against the law, for one thing."

"Wottever," she grunted, her face contorted like a gargoyle as she flicked me the V sign.

I snorted in derision.

"Think that's clever? It'll take a lot more than a rude gesture to rattle my cage, my girl," I said. "We have to be at the clinic in an hour so I suggest that after you've rested those ankles, you hop into the bathroom, freshen up and put on some clean clothes.

"Oh, and another thing," I said as I turned to leave, "I'll be obliged to tell your social worker Janet about this little episode."

I expected some childish retaliation, but when none came, I looked around.

Susan had started to retch and was drooling over her pillow.

"I think I'm going to be ...."

Suddenly she vomited, spewing sick all over her black dress and the yellow bedspread.

"Okay Susan, you're alright," I said, propping her up against a pillow and turning her face to the side so that she didn't choke. "Take deep breaths while I find something to clean you up."

Dashing into the bathroom I filled a plastic bowl with water and Dettol, and grabbed a pile of towels from the airing cupboard.

When I returned to her room, Susan was whimpering and in tears. Suddenly the vulnerable young girl inside her had surfaced.

"Do you normally smoke and drink as much as that?" I asked, placing a cold wet flannel across her sweaty brow.

She shook her head.

"Not as much as all that. And I don't want to ever again."

"So why now?" I probed, stripping off the dirty bedspread.

At first she refused to meet my eye, but then, sheepishly, she opened up.

"You all think you're better than me, everyone does. I can see it from the way you look at me."

Grabbing the hankie I offered, she blew her nose loudly.

"Well it's just me on my own now – with this!" she exclaimed, pointing to her bump.

"It's hard, I know," I said gently. "But let me give you a piece of advice, love. The only thing you should be worrying about now is looking after yourself and that baby inside you.

"Now go and have a nice warm bath and let's get down the clinic for that check-up."

As I gathered up the vomit-covered clothes and bedspread to take downstairs for a soak, Susan lumbered to the bathroom and ran herself a bath.

Half an hour later, there was still no sign of her, so I tapped on the door.

"Susan, could you hurry up please!"

When she finally emerged, she left a cloud of steam in her wake.

I peered inside the bathroom. Not only had Susan not emptied her dirty bath water, there were wet towels strewn all over the bathroom.

"Another bad habit," I muttered under my breath as I flung the sopping wet towels into a pile for my next laundry load.

Then I noticed the sweet citrus smell of mandarin in the air – and an orange bottle rolling around on the floor. It was the Aqua Manda bath foam Bill had given me for my birthday.

Picking it up, I discovered that Susan had used every last drop.

I was furious.

"Susan," I called, waving the empty bottle outside her bedroom door. "You've used up all my bath foam. Surely a few drops would have been enough for one bath?"

Susan looked at me and shrugged.

"Alright, keep your hair on," she said. "I thought it was for everyone. That's how it was at the children's home."

"Well, it would have been nice if you'd asked first," I added, "and I don't think I've heard the word 'sorry' yet."

"Leave me alone," she protested. "I've gotta get ready."

With that, she shut the door in my face.

Later at the clinic, Susan was as nice as pie. Polite and amenable, she let the nurses examine her and take a blood sample without making a fuss. She even smiled when they told her the baby had turned and was almost "cooked" as the chirpy nurse described it.

The following day, I thought a trip to the shops to buy baby bottles and paraphernalia for newborns might spark even more interest and excitement for her unborn child.

But as we wandered around looking at clothes, changing mats and baby powder, Susan was back to her former childish behaviour.

She reminded me of Jekyll and Hyde. One minute she was high-spirited and good-humoured, making silly noises and laughing like a big kid, the next she was belligerent and aggressive if another shopper even looked at her.

"Wot are you starin' at?" she barked when another pregnant woman accidentally glanced in her direction.

"I'm very sorry, love," I said to the startled shopper, steering Susan out of the shop. "Her hormones are running riot today!"

It took all my self-control not to march Susan straight home.

The final straw came when we visited Mothercare.

As I marvelled at all the beautiful, pastel-coloured baby outfits, feeling nostalgic about my three newborns, Susan suddenly vanished.

I searched the entire length of the shop and, panicking now, approached a sales assistant.

"Have you seen the young girl who was with me just now?" I asked. "She's heavily pregnant, with blonde hair and wearing a black dress."

The girl shook her head.

Just as I was about to leave the shop to find a call box to ring Janet, I heard giggling from a changing cubicle.

"Is that you, Susan?" I called through the curtain. "I've been looking for you everywhere!"

"Come in and have a look, Jeanie," she said.

I pulled back the curtain to find her wearing a long, billowing red maternity dress with a big bow at the front.

"That looks, um, lovely, Susan," I said, surprised at her vivid and rather twee choice.

She turned to look at her reflection from every angle in the mirror, smiling broadly.

"But you're due to have the baby soon," I said. "Do you think you need that dress now? It's baby things we came out for, really."

Susan pouted like a sulky child.

I looked at the price tag on the dress. It was in the sale.

"All right, you can have it," I relented, secretly relieved that it would mean seeing Susan in a colour other than black.

But just as I was about to take the dress to the till, Susan's face crumpled and she let out an almighty laugh.

"I'm joking, Jeanie," she giggled. "I'd *never* wear that in a million years!"

She had taken me for a fool and I fell for it.

"That's it, Susan," I said, stoney-faced. "Home. Now."

She couldn't understand why I wasn't laughing too.

"It was just a joke," she whined. "What's the big deal?"

It wasn't really her fault, I reminded myself on the frosty journey home. Susan was so stunted in her emotional development that she had no empathy and was insensitive to other people's feelings. But I was so upset by her cruel trick, by her throwing kindness back in my face, that I couldn't bring myself to speak to her at all on the way back.

By the time we arrived home, she was shamefaced.

"Sorry, Jeanie," she said, bringing me a cup of tea that she'd made with hot water from the tap – the method she'd used as a kid.

I knew she was sincerely sorry I was upset, even if she didn't really understand why. But in between her calmer moments, Susan's moods were a real problem.

One rainy Saturday the kids invited her to play Monopoly on the kitchen table. Bill and I watched discreetly from the sidelines, cautiously optimistic that this game would forge a few bonds between them.

However, despite a promising start where they all had fun choosing their tokens – Susan insisted on having the shoe, or what she called with a cackle, "the old boot" – our guest found it hard to play by the rules.

After landing on Stevie's Park Lane for the umpteenth time, she was obliged to pay up again.

"No, I'm not going to pay you, Stevie," she said petulantly.

"You've got to pay, that's how this game works," he reasoned. "Anyway, it's not real money – it's only a game."

But Susan shook her head.

"I can't, I've run out of cash," she lied, hiding a wad of pink and green notes behind her back.

Outraged by her dishonesty, Stevie tried to grab the money from her hand.

Yet Susan stood her ground.

"I don't like this game any more," she yelled. "It's stupid!"

She stood up and flicked her hand underneath the board, scattering all the little green and red plastic houses and silver tokens over the floor.

The children looked at her, aghast.

They had squabbled over games before, but Susan's outburst was on a whole other level.

As she stormed up to her room, I followed her.

"You need to try and control your temper," I told her. "I understand that your hormones must be running riot and you're scared about becoming a mum, but you can't get away with lashing out when things don't go your way."

Just as she was about to answer back, I cut her off.

"Take a deep breath and count to ten next time you feel anger brewing up inside you," I said firmly. "If that doesn't work, take yourself away from what's making you livid, leave the room for ten minutes, anything but blowing up."

"But he..."

"I don't want to hear it, Susan." I interjected. "Stevie didn't deserve that. The bottom line is that if you keep kicking off, you'll drive away your friends. What's more, you can't behave like that when you're baby comes along. You need to stay calm for that.

"Don't come back down until you've cooled off," I continued. "Then you will apologise."

In the kitchen Stevie and the girls gathered up pieces from the game and put them safely back in the box.

"She's crazy!" railed Stevie. "That's the last time I ask her to play a game with us."

"She's scary," said Sophie, taking her older sister's hand. Sarah nodded vigorously.

Although I loathed seeing my children distressed by Susan's dramatics, I gathered them around me to try and help them understand why Susan had her temper tantrums.

"What Susan did was very wrong," I said. "And yes, she does seem scary when she shouts and kicks off. But the thing you might not realise is that she's very frightened, too."

"About the baby?" asked Sarah.

"Yes, love," I said. "And she knows this baby will be born very soon. She doesn't have a mam and dad to help her through it, see. So I'm – we're – taking their place for a bit."

The kids nodded solemnly, before wandering off to play another game together.

Bill and I knew that, despite my pep talk with Susan, this wouldn't be the last time she flared up.

However, after the Monopoly outburst, she kept a low profile, fitting in with our household routine and putting on a polite front with us all or quietly sulking.

It was such a contrast to her former behaviour that I couldn't help feeling uneasy, as if the bubble – and Susan's temper – was about to burst.

Sure enough, it happened at the worst possible time: when Bill's mum came over that Sunday.

Honest to a fault, Ivy and her direct manner grated on Susan from the moment they were introduced.

As Ivy looked our newcomer up and down, noting her bleached hair, short skirt and red lipstick, she gave her verdict.

"You're a pretty girl," she said, "underneath all that make-up."

This was like red rag to a bull to Susan, whose smile morphed into a scowl.

"Yeah, well I don't wanna look like a fogey just yet, thank you, gran," Susan retorted, waving her arm at Ivy's tweed skirt and her Sunday-best hat.

"What a cheek," said Ivy, raising her eyebrows.

Letting out a low whistle, she then turned to look at Bill and me.

"You got your work cut out with this one," she remarked, imperiously handing me her hat and coat. "A bit of a wild cat, she."

To be fair, it was Ivy who had provoked this spat, and although Susan should not have retaliated, it looked like a one-all score to me.

Still sore from her clash with Ivy, Susan sat sulking on her own in the corner, while Stevie and the girls played cards.

I'd learnt that during her moody moments it was best to leave Susan to calm down and emerge of her own accord rather than force her to join in.

Meanwhile, Bill prepared our Sunday roast and, in time-honoured tradition, poured Ivy and me some pre-dinner drinks.

"Two Martini and lemonades coming up," he said breezily, popping ice cubes and colourful umbrella cocktail decorations into our glasses. "Dinner will be ready in an hour."

As Ivy and I chatted about our week, I didn't register Susan approach Sarah and Sophie and whisper something in their ears.

The trio then slipped out of the sitting room to go upstairs, and all that I could hear was the sound of their distant laughter.

When the three of them finally came down for dinner, I was flabbergasted by the sight that greeted us.

Parading into the dining room in their swimsuits, Sarah and Sophie struck a pose so that Ivy, Bill and I could admire their garish makeovers. The vivid pink lipstick, sparkly blue eyeshadow and scarlet nail polish were, I realised, all courtesy of Susan.

"What do you think?" asked Sarah, pleased as punch with her new look. "We're playing beauty contests, like Miss World."

Smiling with pride, Sophie gave us a twirl.

Watching my two girls, who were both blossoming into young women, put on this inappropriate display made me feel sick.

Yet they were totally unaware that this was more than just an innocent makeover: Susan had sexualised them in the way that she had been.

"Crikey, you're a bit young for this sort of thing, girls!" gasped Bill in disapproval. "I think you need to put some clothes on."

I was so stunned I didn't know what to say to them. Even Ivy was speechless!

While Bill and I squirmed at Susan's handiwork, it was no doubt Ivy's response – pursed lips and an expression that looked as if she had been sucking on a lemon – that put the gloating smirk on Susan's face. After her unfavourable comment about Susan's make-up, this was the mischievous girl's revenge.

She'd got us over a barrel. If we became angry we'd just upset Sarah and Sophie over something that wasn't their fault.

"It's, um, very bright," I said, choosing my words carefully. "You can keep it on just this once in the house, but you're too young to wear it outside. And put on some clothes right now. It's too cold to be eating in a swimsuit."

Although I had occasionally let 14 year-old Sarah wear pale pink nail varnish and play with the teenage beauty set we'd given her for Christmas, there was no way I would have allowed her and her younger sister to go out in the gaudy get-up Susan had dreamed up.

Looking at their innocent faces plastered in that stuff was a sad reminder how Susan had been wearing it on a daily basis since she wasn't much older than Sophie. Unlike the novelty and fun it presented to the girls, it had a darker connotation for her. Mark, and no doubt other men, had used it as part of a grooming technique on poor young Susan, but she had no-one like me to step in and stop them from stealing her innocence.

As sympathetic as I felt for her ordeal, however, I had to prevent her from using Sarah and Sophie as pawns to express her anger.

After tea, while Bill was driving Ivy home, I discreetly took Susan to one side.

"I know what you did back there," I told her. "You were angry with Ivy so you used the girls to make a point."

"I've no idea what you're on about," she shrugged. "They wear them swimsuits at the beach, don't they? What's the difference?"

"Yes, to swim and make sandcastles," I said. "Not strutting about in make-up – there's a huge difference, young lady."

Susan stared impassively at the floor.

"Try and be good, just for one day, please," I pleaded.

"I don't want to be good!" she hissed, curling her lip in disdain. "Good girls are boring! Look at your Sophie and Sarah, right little goody-goodies. What they need is a good punching."

I recoiled at the force of her vitriol.

Suddenly, she was crying, deep, heart-wrenching sobs that wracked through her and touched my soul.

"Come here, love," I said. I wrapped my arms around Susan as her entire body heaved in despair.

"It's not fair!"

"Let it all out," I whispered. She buried her face in my sleeve and wept.

When she came up for air, I handed her a tissue and stroked her hair. She was just a kid, a lost, lonely child whose life so far had been blighted by the adults who should have loved and protected her. Instead they used and abused her for their own selfish ends.

"So tell me, love," I coaxed gently. "What happened?"

Susan sniffed and took a deep breath.

"They used to make me…" she began, her voice trailing off before she plucked up the courage to continue. "They made me walk around the flat in a bra and pants when the men came over."

"Who, love, who made you?"

"Dad mainly, and me mam," she said bleakly. "The men gave dad money after.

"At first it was just to look. Then they gave dad more money to touch."

Hearing what those parents did made my blood boil, but I couldn't let it show.

"Anything else, love?" I asked, trying to control the quake of emotion in my voice.

"Yeah," she said flatly. "They made me put all this make-up on and go round to each man. I had to touch them."

"Did they… rape you, Susan?"

She shook her head.

"No, I wouldn't. I screamed and kicked out… that's why dad beat me up and I couldn't go to school."

I felt sick to the stomach.

"How old were you then, Susan? Can you remember?"

She nodded.

"I was 13," she said. "It was on my 13th birthday."

Teenage Birth

Susan and I turned a dramatic corner for the better after she opened up to me about the horrific sexual and emotional abuse she had endured.

I filed a report to Carol and Janet, leaving the legal implications of what I'd been told in their court, while I focused on Susan and her baby.

She needed me more than ever as her due date approached and, for the first time, she listened attentively as I spoke to her about what to expect during childbirth.

"Will it hurt, Jeanie?" she asked as I popped into her room to say goodnight. "I'm scared about that."

I've always believed that honesty is the best policy in matters like this. When I was a girl, speaking about all the gory details of having a baby, from the conception to the birth, were practically forbidden, especially for unmarried women. So first-time mums had no idea what was going to happen when the time came.

"It will be painful, Susan," I replied. "But the weird thing is you forget all about that when you see your baby for the first time."

"You've done it three times, though, Jeanie," said Susan. "What was it like?"

The truth was that the first time I gave birth, aged 18, I had a long and painful labour and thought I was going to die.

Yet with Sophie and Stevie, my body seemed to know what to do. Although it obviously hurt again to push those babies out, giving birth was shorter, more pleasurable somehow, and I had Bill by my side, cheering me on. I didn't think it would help Susan to hear that my first time was by far the most traumatic. There is such a thing as being too honest.

"We should just wait and see, love," I said. "No point expecting the worst – or the best – and getting worked up about it. Let's focus on what's in front of us now."

Susan stared at her huge tummy as if it was a separate entity, not part of her body at all.

"It's massive," she gasped. "How is this baby gonna come out?"

"It will come out the same way it went in," I explained.

She screwed up her face, trying to imagine how it would happen.

"There's not enough room for that, Jeanie," she complained. "It's just not... big enough."

I picked up my well-thumbed book about pregnancy and childbirth and opened it to show her a picture of how her bump looked inside.

"Look, Susan, it's not all baby in there," I reassured her. "There's also amniotic fluid and a placenta that feeds the baby its oxygen and nutrients. Your little one will weigh about 7 or 8lbs, I should think."

Susan still looked terrified.

"I just don't think it will be able to squeeze out," she said.

I opened the book at the page where it describes how the cervix dilates to allow the baby to squeeze through.

"A bit of light reading before you go to sleep," I smiled.

With a wide yawn, Susan nodded and put the book on her bedside table.

"Don't worry too much, love," I said gently as I switched off her light. "You'll be taken care of by the doctors and nurses, and I'll be with you every step of the way."

As I drifted off to sleep that night, memories of giving birth to Sarah filled my head. One afternoon I was in the box room at Norma's, putting up the pair of curtains I'd just run up on the old Singer, when my waters broke and my contractions began.

I'd never felt pain like it. The excruciating, relentless twisting sensation in my tummy was so overwhelming that I collapsed on to the wooden floor.

"Norma!" I screamed. "Help me!"

This vivid recollection woke me up with a start.

Still panting in frantic rhythm with my pounding heart, I could feel beads of cold sweat trickling down my face.

Suddenly I heard a yelp. Was I still dreaming? Or was it the sound of a vixen calling to her cubs outside?

I lay still, hearing only Bill's soft breathing next to me.

But then, there it was again. This time it was louder, shriller, the cry of pain. There was no mistaking that sound.

It was coming from Susan's room.

I glanced at the clock: it was 3am.

Wide awake now, I jumped up and fumbled for my dressing gown.

Bill stirred beside me.

"Everything okay, Jeanie?" he asked sleepily.

"I think it's started."

"What's started?" he murmured.

"I think Susan's having contractions," I said. "She's a bit early, but it's time."

I must have sprinted across the landing to Susan's room When I flung open the door, I saw that she was on her knees, clinging to the side of her bed and groaning.

"Don't worry, love, I'm here!" I said, crouching by her side. "When did it start, do you know?"

"About ten minutes ago," she gasped. "I thought I needed to go to the bog. When I stood up, a load of water gushed out. Then I felt my tummy twist and I was sick. I fell over."

In between the deep breaths, she was crying and gripping the bedspread until her knuckles turned white.

"I'm gonna die, Jeanie!" she wailed, looking at me with fear in her eyes.

"No, love," I said, rubbing her back. "We're going to get you to hospital now, and you're going to have your baby."

The clamour had woken up the kids and when I looked behind me, I saw three concerned faces peering around the door.

"Mam, what's happening?" asked Sarah, her voice quivering in panic. "Is Susan all right?"

"Yes, love," I said. "Could you go and get an empty plastic bowl and a flannel soaked in cold water from the bathroom, please. Sophie, Stevie, help dad put a hospital bag together for Susan. Nice and quick please, loves."

They dashed off to find Bill, who was up and dressed, and searching for the car keys.

When Sarah returned with the flannel, she crouched next to Susan and started mopping her brow.

"It's all right," she said soothingly, while I ran back to my bedroom and flung on some clothes. "We'll look after you."

On my way back to Susan's room I passed Bill on the landing.

"I'll drive her there," I said. "You stay here with the kids."

Bill nodded and passed me the ignition key and the bag.

"The roads are quiet at this time of night, so it should only take 15 minutes to get there."

When I returned to Susan's room, she had been sick in the bowl and was trying to stand up.

"Oh god," she shrieked. "I need the toilet right now, I'm gonna poo myself."

"No Susan, that's the baby you can feel."

She looked alarmed.

"What, it's not coming out that way, is it?"

At that moment, another contraction kicked in and she crumpled.

"I hate it," she moaned, weeping and raging simultaneously. "I wish I'd never let that bastard touch me!"

In the car on the way to hospital, Susan was gripped with pain, and groaning at every bump in the road.

Winding down the window, she retched into the breeze.

"Nearly there," I assured her as we raced through the dark empty streets.

"How did you do this – three times?" she screeched.

"It's what we women do," I said. "We've been doing this since the dawn of time. And a lot of women do it more than three times."

Susan looked at me in horrified disbelief.

"But I'm not a woman," she cried. "I'm a girl!"

"You're not the first girl to go through this and you won't be the last. I was only a couple of years older than you when I did it, you know."

She glanced at me sideways, looking at me in a new light.

"Oh, that was nothing compared to what my mum did," I said. "She had five of us. All in her bed at home with just a local midwife delivering her babes."

My poor mum Mary – worn out by pregnancy, childbirth, poverty, and drudgery. No control over her own body. But in the end it was cancer that got her. Her life was snuffed out just like that.

"Try to take deep breaths," I urged Susan as I pulled into the hospital car park. "It'll help."

She clung to me for dear life as we staggered into the maternity ward.

"Please don't leave me, Jeanie," she pleaded, as a nurse led her into the room where she would give birth.

"Are you her mum?" asked the matron who was filling in the official paperwork.

"Yes," I began. "I mean, no, I'm her foster mum."

Susan clutched my hand as I hurried to her side. Around her, a group of nurses, who had seen it all a hundred times before, calmly prepared for the delivery.

"Oh, she's a screamer, this one," said one of the older nurses. "Calm down, child. You'll wake the whole ward!"

The level of sympathy for girls like Susan in those days was a lot lower than you'd experience today, but I leapt to her defence anyway.

"She's only 15," I pointed out. "She's never done this before."

The nurse raised her eyebrows and tutted.

"Let's see how far she's dilated."

Despite the frequency of her contractions, Susan's body wasn't ready for her to start pushing and we had to wait to let nature take its course.

It was another hour before she was encouraged to push. Finally, six hours later, exhausted and wrung out from trying to deliver her baby, Susan was too weak to push any more.

Eventually, she had to give birth by forceps. Her bouncing baby boy bawled his way into the world later that morning.

"Would you like to hold him?" the nurse asked Susan after wrapping him in a blanket.

But she was too traumatised to do much more than glance at the chubby little bruiser, who had a mop of fair hair like his mum and was screaming for his first feed.

Suddenly, as they were waiting for the afterbirth to come away, Susan started to haemorrhage. It was a bloodbath.

I held the baby as a doctor rushed in and tried to contract her womb while an emergency medical team surrounded her.

"What's happening, Jeanie?" whispered Susan, turning her head to look at me. "Everything's going black."

I was sick with fear. A woman in the town where I grew up had died like this during childbirth, leaving four kids without a mother. Surely this couldn't happen here, in a modern hospital, to a girl of 15?

"Don't go to sleep, Susan," I pleaded. "Keep your eyes open, keep breathing. Talk to me."

"I'm cold," she said, barely audible, as a medical team fought to save her life. "Take Jack over there. I don't want him to see this."

Jack, she said. Despite appearing to be in denial about her baby before he was born, Susan had secretly chosen a name for him.

I cried softly with him in my arms as I walked up and down outside the room, rocking him to sleep and praying that his mum would live.

Susan had lost so much blood that she needed a transfusion.

After calling Bill on the hospital payphone, I sat with her all night, stroking her hair and feeding Jack with a pipette of special formula milk whenever he cried.

Too frail to even hold or look at her new baby, Susan shivered and asked for another blanket.

"You've lost a lot of blood, love," I explained, piling several on to her bed. "That's why you're cold."

Although I didn't tell her this at the time, the doctor grimly told me that she was lucky to be alive. If she'd tried to give birth at home, she wouldn't have survived.

That afternoon, Bill brought the kids to visit, with flowers and chocolates for Susan and a beautiful blue outfit for baby Jack.

"Thanks everyone," she smiled, still weak from her ordeal. "I wanna come home soon."

Without even thinking, she'd called our house "home"'and I was surprised at how much this moved me.

Susan had to stay in hospital for four days to recover, and in between looking after my own family, I would spend as much time with her as I could during visiting hours.

Despite the trauma she had suffered, the impatient nurses fully expected her to breastfeed little Jack.

"I can't do it and I don't like it," she complained. "It hurts and he won't stay on."

I asked her to show me what she had been doing.

For a girl who'd flaunted her cleavage often enough before her baby was born, she suddenly seemed shy about getting a boob out for what nature intended.

"Don't look," she protested as milk gushed through her cotton pyjama top before she could suckle Jack.

She was all fingers and thumbs as she tried to latch him on.

"It feels weird," she grumbled. "Can't we just give him a bottle?"

Mum's the Word

Trying to teach Susan how to be a mother to Jack was, to put it mildly, a challenge.

As she regained her strength at home following her life-or-death ordeal, she regained her chippiness, too, and it felt as if we'd lost most of the progress we had ever made.

At first she would half-heartedly feed and change her baby, but made such a hash of it that I would invariably take over.

It was the mess, the monotony and the relentlessness of the routine that she couldn't quite grasp.

She avoided breastfeeding as much as she could and would make excuses about why she didn't change Jack's nappy often enough.

"It stinks, Jeanie," she grumbled, her hand over her nose, as I showed her what to do with a soaking-wet soiled nappy – and how to put on a fresh one.

Not only was she still pretty squeamish, she was clueless, too.

"You'll get used to the pong," I laughed. "Nappies are easy once you know what order to do it all in."

Placing Jack on his changing mat, I guided her through the medley of cotton wool and warm water, baby cream and talcum powder, fresh towelling nappy and safety pins, and finally the protective plastic pants.

"Pop the soiled nappy in that bucket please, love," I said casually, observing what her reaction would be. "We're going to have to wash it in sanitising powder and boiling water so that we can use it again. Babies get through quite a few nappies in a day."

It was a mucky, tedious task and I didn't blame Susan for the daunted expression on her face.

But the boring yet essential routine of looking after a baby was a fact of life that she would need to take on board if she was prepared to become a full time mum.

That first hurdle on day one was complete, but my task of guiding her through the ups and downs, the sleepless nights, the crying and the never-ending feeds had only just begun.

Showing Susan how to bathe Jack was an important part of it, too. Placing him on a changing mat on the floor, I knelt down beside him and rolled up my sleeve.

"This is how you test the temperature," I explained, dipping my elbow into the water in his plastic baby bath. "It has to be just right for the baby."

Carefully lowering Jack into the tub, I showed Susan how I kept my hand firmly underneath him for support.

Then, as the warm water swirled all around him, he began to gurgle and kick his chubby little legs with glee.

"Aah, that's so sweet," said Susan, lighting up with enthusiasm for the first time since he'd been born.

Within just half an hour of his bath, however, Jack let us know with a piercing cry that he needed changing again.

Putting her hands over her ears, Susan looked to me for help.

"Come on, love," I said, chivvying her along. "I'll watch you put his nappy on and take over if you get stuck."

In a cautious attempt, she managed to take the nappy off, but didn't dispose of it quickly enough. As Jack wriggled impatiently, keen to be rid of the soiled square of towel, he kicked out and a yellow-brown mess splashed over his legs and on to Susan's hands.

"Yuck!" she squealed, jumping in revulsion. "I'm not going near that again."

With a sigh, I handed her a cloth to clean herself up and took over.

While Susan was understandably dismayed by dirty nappies, she didn't have much interest in giving Jack his night feed either. Whenever the poor little mite cried in the cot next to her, she'd pull the covers over her head and yell, "Shuddup!"

It all came to a head when he was a few weeks old and I had to traipse into her room – again – to have a word.

"Susan, he's hungry," I said gently. "If you feed him, he will stop crying and then everyone, including you, can get some sleep."

"Don't care. Get him out of here!" she hissed like a petulant child, before bursting into hysterical tears.

By then, Jack's piercing cries had woken up the kids and they were standing bleary-eyed on the landing.

"Is baby Jack all right, Mummy?" asked Sophie. "Does he want a toy to cuddle?"

"Shall I fetch some nappies from the bathroom?" Sarah chipped in.

"He's so-o-o loud," Stevie complained grumpily, sticking his fingers in his ears.

"Go back to bed, all of you," I said. "You've got school in the morning. Don't worry about Jack. Susan and I are sorting him out."

Yawning in unison, my three youngsters nodded and padded back to bed.

Bill had woken up, too, and after yet another night of sleep deprivation, he was none too pleased.

"Ok, I'll make up a bottle," he said grumpily. "But this is the last time, Susan. That little fella is right there next to you; can't you just pick him up and find out what he wants?"

It was the first time Bill had ever told her off, really, and Susan was stunned. She started to cry again, but it was all down to self-pity.

"I want my life to go back to how it was before," she wailed. "I don't want to be a mum, I can't do it."

Wearily, I sat in the nursing chair and fed Jack the bottle that Bill had just made. I had always loved those night feeds when I was a new mum. Yes, I was so tired

I almost had to prop open my eyes with matchsticks, but it was a magical time: sitting there in the silence, looking at those trusting eyes gazing up at you, feeling their tiny fingers curled around yours. Just you and your baby.

What Susan didn't get yet was that, no matter how tired you are, how grumpy, it is insignificant compared with the overwhelming love you have for your child. I wanted to help her find that love – if she had it in her.

As Susan slept, I finished feeding Jack, winded him, changed his nappy and settled him back in his cot. I was exhausted and it wasn't me who needed to bond with the baby: something had to change.

After the kids had gone to school the next morning, I sat Susan down at the kitchen table for a serious talk.

"I don't understand what's going on in your mind," I said. "You had a lucky escape in hospital and now you have a beautiful baby boy. But instead of looking after him, all you seem to want to do is watch TV all day."

Susan refused to meet my gaze.

"I did it for a bit, but it's boring, I can't do anything else."

I shook my head in disbelief.

"Sure, of course babies need to be fed and changed all day and all night," I said. "They're little feeding, sleeping, pooing and crying machines and it never stops. But there's all the good stuff, too: don't you just love giving him a cuddle, a nuzzle as you rock him to sleep?"

At that moment, the distinctive smell of soiled nappy wafted past.

"Jack's nappy needs changing," I reminded her.

"But I only changed him an hour ago!"

"And you'll probably do it again in another hour, Susan. How would you feel if you were completely helpless, if you had to lie in your own poo and the person who is supposed to love and care for you never fed you?"

That struck a chord. Susan did understand exactly how that felt because she'd experienced it herself. She knew only too well what it was like to be hungry and neglected.

A silence descended over us as the parallel clicked into place.

"I'll sort out his nappy," she said.

The next 24 hours would be the litmus test for Susan, her chance to prove either her commitment to motherhood – or her rejection of it. The way she behaved next would determine whether or not she would keep Jack.

"You're still a young girl and have your whole life ahead of you," I said. "No-one will judge or think any less of you if you aren't sure it's what you really want."

A flicker of indignation lit her eyes. Susan looked at me and insisted, "No, I want Jack. I won't be a mum who walks away from her kid."

I was pleased to hear her say that she wanted Jack. Once she'd made her promise, Susan got off to a good start. Judging by the peace and quiet that descended from upstairs after Jack woke up crying from his nap, I guessed that she must have picked him up.

After this huge first step, she began breastfeeding, despite her embarrassment, taking Jack to her room so that she could do it in private.

However, one afternoon, when I gently opened her bedroom door and peeked in, Susan was asleep on the nursing chair midfeed. Jack was nodding off too, his rosy cheek scrunched up against her shoulder. In this precarious position he could have fallen on the floor while Susan was having her 40 winks.

"It's best to let him lie down, now," I whispered, helping her place Jack into his cot, as he snuffled and twitched his button nose.

"You also need to be careful that he doesn't expect to fall asleep on you every time he has a feed, otherwise you won't be able to get a single thing done."

Susan grinned.

With a marked improvement in her care of Jack every day, I really believed we were making a breakthrough.

One beautiful sunny morning, Susan even felt confident enough to take him out for a walk in the pram by herself.

"We're going to the park to feed the ducks, Jeanie," she said cheerfully. "I'll bring some dry bread with me."

"Do you want me to come too?" I asked. "We could go for a coffee at that funny little hut down there."

"Oh, no, you get on with what you have to do here," she replied, hurrying away. "Jack and I will be fine."

Susan was gone for hours.

When lunchtime came and went, I felt mildly concerned by her absence. But by the time the kids came home from school, she still hadn't returned and panic was beginning to set in.

Then I found out where she was.

"Mam, me and Sophie have just seen Susan," said Sarah, sounding worried. "She's down the park…"

"Still? She's been there all day. What was she doing?"

Sarah hesitated and looked at Sophie.

"She's with a group of lads."

My pulse started to race in anger and fear.

"What lads?" I demanded. "Where's Jack, did you see him?"

"In his pram by the pond," said Sophie. "And Susan was sitting on that lad's lap and kissing."

"Did he have dark blond hair?"

Sarah nodded sheepishly.

"Did they see you, love?"

"No, I don't think so," replied Sarah. "The trees were in the way."

I was devastated. By picking up her relationship with this Mark, Susan had not only betrayed us, she was putting her baby son – and herself – in danger.

Bill was livid when I told him.

He was on the verge of storming down the park to bring Susan and Jack back, but I had to stop him.

"They might have knives," I warned him. "If Susan's not back within the hour, we'll call Janet and the police."

Half an hour later, Susan casually ambled in, with Jack asleep in his pram.

Her eyes were still sparkling from her secret liaison – until she saw the expression on my face. She realised immediately that I knew.

Instead of facing the music, she ran upstairs with Jack in her arms and slammed her bedroom door.

I followed her up.

"Susan," I said, tapping on her door and trying to sound calm. "Can I come in?"

"Yeah," she replied. "But you won't change my mind, Jeanie."

"About what?" I replied, stepping inside.

"About me and Mark," she said flatly. "We love each other and I'm gonna take Jack with me to live with him."

I was stunned.

"When was this decided? I had no idea you were seeing him again."

"Today," she said. "I bumped into him at the park."

"So after everything you've been through, the progress you've made, you're prepared to ruin it all for this, this... petty criminal?" I managed not to give voice to the names I was calling him in my head. "Where would you even live?"

"In the squat."

I shook my head in disbelief.

"You can't bring Jack up in a squat. He's just a baby."

Susan just stared back at me, unmoved by the tears starting to well up in my eyes.

How Could She?

That evening, I rang Carol and Janet and told them of the devastating development.

"This is very serious," said Janet, with her unerring ability to state the obvious. "We'll be around first thing to talk this through. Try to make sure that Susan doesn't leave the house at all between now and tomorrow morning. Her safety – and Jack's – could depend on it."

That night I couldn't get to sleep, I couldn't silence all the anxious questions whirling around in my head.

How could we keep Susan and her baby safe? Was it my fault, as a foster mum, that it hadn't worked out with her? I'd thought it had been going so well between us, that we were finally making headway, but my judgment was evidently skewed.

I was just drifting off when a creaking floorboard on the landing woke me up with a start. The alarm clock told me it was midnight.

Then there was another sound. Voices. Whispers rising and falling, as if in conflict, coming from our porch outside.

Who was down there at this time of night?

Straining to listen, I heard a man's voice, domineering and persistent, then the sound of a woman.

My worst fears were realised: Susan was talking to Mark at the door. Then I heard footsteps on the stairs, followed by the sound of Susan closing her bedroom door.

Suddenly I felt sick with dread. She must have come back up to fetch her things to do a midnight flit with Mark. Was she taking her baby?

Jack, perhaps sensing his mother was leaving him, started to cry. Then the sound of her footsteps coming down the stairs.

"So this is it… the end of the line," I whispered to myself. "How could she? The familiar pull of her old life was just too strong."

Then the front door slammed so hard that it made the letterbox rattle. I heard their footsteps racing down the front path. A car door shut with a decisive bang.

Jumping out of bed, I dashed to my bedroom window, pulled back the net curtains and peered through. It was Mark's car parked outside and although I couldn't see anyone sitting inside, I knew it was him, showing off in front of Susan as he deliberately revved up his engine loud enough to wake the entire neighbourhood.

"She's gone," I said in disbelief under my breath as tears of anger and sadness pricked my eyes at the recklessness of what she was doing. It was then that noticed how quiet the house was. "What about Jack? Where's the baby?"

The car screeched around the corner and they were gone.

My voice was choked with emotion as I said to Bill, "Susan's left, gone off with Mark and I don't know if she's taken Jack."

"What? You have got to be joking!" Bill groaned shaking his head. "Surely she wouldn't do that now?"

But as I opened Jack's door, I couldn't believe my eyes.

There was Susan, silently weeping, with Jack in her arms.

"That's it – Mark's gone," she wailed. "He made me choose. My life is really screwed now. What 'ave I done? I'm on my own."

Overwhelmed with relief, I put my arms around her and Jack and held them close.

"No love, you made the right choice. I'll help you get through this. Take it from me, there's a better life out there for you and little Jack – with or without a man."

This wasn't what Susan wanted to hear right now.

Pulling away, she shot me a look of contempt, and sneered, "What do you know? With your perfect little home and your perfect little family. I know what you really think about me. You wouldn't even talk to me if you weren't being paid to do it."

Her words cut me to the quick. Holding back the tears, I looked her in the eye.

"Susan, I know exactly how it feels to be on your own with a baby," I said. "To have no one to turn to, no family to help, no idea what happens next. I know because it happened to me, too. I was in exactly the same situation as you."

She stared back at me in stunned silence.

"You're not alone, Susan," I continued. "I'm here for you and want to help you so much. Will you let me?"

She nodded uncertainly.

Bill popped his head round the door.

"Are you both okay?"

"Don't worry, love. We're fine. Go back to bed."

I took Susan downstairs to the kitchen, plugged in the electric fire and put the kettle on.

As we sipped our mugs of tea, Jack sleeping soundly under a blanket on the sofa between us, I took a deep breath and told Susan my story...

I was 16 years old when I left the convent, and it was one of the happiest days of my life. I'd waited for that moment of freedom for so long, like a prisoner about to be set free after serving a six-year sentence.

Sister Gertrude, or Gertrude the Gorgon as we called her, told us we should feel lucky and grateful for the spiritual guidance we had received.

What a joke that was! Her so-called spiritual guidance hadn't brought us any closer to God – it had been like some kind of cruel purgatory.

At a special leaving ceremony, she presented us all with a book of prayer, instructing us upon our departure to go forth and serve our communities like good girls, not the wicked girls we'd been up until now.

I was relieved to be going home to be with my Dad, who was becoming increasingly frail.

Despite my experience at the convent, I'd go to church every Sunday and it was here that I met the man who would change the course of my life.

A so-called devout Catholic and respected member of the community, he was married with two children and was a friend of my father. On the face of it, he seemed like a nice fella who took what appeared to be a paternal interest in me.

However, as the two of us walked home from Mass one Sunday, his tone changed.

"You're a very attractive girl, Jeanie," he said. "And you've grown up a lot since I last saw you. You have a boyfriend now, I suppose?"

I blushed with embarrassment. There was something in his tone that was overly familiar. And, as we strolled through the fields, he looked at me with an intensity that made me feel uncomfortable.

"No, I don't have a boyfriend," I said, looking away. "I'm not interested."

This suddenly felt uncomfortable. Not right... I couldn't wait to get away from him, to get home. My pace quickened, but so did his.

As I climbed a wooden stile, he grabbed me, pulling me down. He started mauling me, putting his hands all over the top of my dress and then, after he threw me to the ground... underneath.

"Get off me!" I yelled. "I'll tell my dad!"

"Your dad?" he sneered. "He won't believe you, Jeanie. Nobody will. Who'd listen to the stories of a silly little girl like you over someone like me?"

I struggled with all my strength and when I tried to knee him in the balls, he yanked my hair and put his hand across my mouth.

"Shut up, you harlot," he hissed. "I doubt you're a virgin anyway, you convent girls love a bit fun, eh?"

Afterwards, I lay among the brambles, my white cotton dress ripped and dirty with grass and blood stains. He calmly stood up, zipped up his trousers and lit a cigarette.

"Wearing a dress like that, you knew what you were doing," he muttered under his breath. "You tempted me, Jeanie, going out looking like that. It's your fault, I responded because I'm only human."

Then, flicking his fag butt away, he added, "Girls like you need to control their lust. You get men into trouble."

I was too numb with shame and shock to move.

How could that act of brutality have been my fault? Yes, my dress was tight in places, but that's because it was two years old and I couldn't afford to buy a new one.

Somehow I knew that if I'd been wearing an old sack-cloth, he would have done the same. But still I felt a terrible shame.

"I won't tell your dad what you've done," he told me, as if he was being magnanimous. "But you must keep quiet about this, too. I have a standing in this town and if it comes out what happened between us here, you'd be branded an adulteress. Your reputation will be in tatters. And everyone knows that no man will marry spoiled goods."

Once I'd staggered home I burned the dress. I didn't tell a soul and I managed to make excuses so that I never had to return to that church again.

A month later I realised that I'd missed my period. I didn't know what to do, who to turn to, who to tell, so I told no-one. I thought that if I did nothing, it would go away.

I was in denial like you were, Susan.

You see, there was no way I could have even considered having an abortion. Abortion is forbidden, a sin if you're a Catholic like me, and so is adultery. While I was forced to commit one against my will, I certainly wasn't prepared to commit the other.

I was in a Catch-22 situation though, Susan. My community would never have accepted me as an unmarried mother, and I wouldn't countenance giving my child to the convent – I saw how much the nuns despised and abused the poor offspring of women like me.

I was pregnant and in turmoil, so I plucked up the courage to tell the vicious bastard who'd put me in this predicament in the first place.

One evening I waited in the church porch to tell him.

"How do I know it's mine?" he said, looking at me – and my expanding tummy – with contempt. "You let me do it, you probably let others, too."

I was speechless and in tears.

"I didn't let you. You made me!"

Terrified that his disgusting secret would come to light, he paid me off. Shoving a wad of notes into my hand, he said, "Get out of this town, Jeanie. If you stay, you and your little bastard will be drummed out anyway."

I didn't want his guilt money and threw it at him, the notes fluttering like confetti, and he laughed in my face. "Pride, is it? Don't you think it's a bit late for that? You're in no position to be throwing away good money. Do you want your bastard to starve, too?" When he left, I fell onto my knees and picked up every last note.

That's when I packed a few belongings and caught a ferry across the Irish Sea to England, where nobody would know me and my secret was safe. I told my Dad I had a job over here.

It was a struggle, though, Susan. Emotionally and financially. But then Norma found me one day, praying in the church, and she saved me. She took me in out of the kindness of her heart, gave me a home and looked after me. Norma was my guardian angel and I don't know what I would have done without her. She helped me through it all, Susan, just like I'm helping you.

The Good Mum

Susan saw me in a new light after I told her what had happened to me in Ireland. "Do you ever think about the…"

She wasn't quite sure what word she should use, so I said it for her.

"The rape? Hardly ever now. I won't let that low-life possess any part of me, including my mind, again."

Thinking about her own hideous experience of sexual abuse, Susan nodded, "I'm gonna do the same as you, Jeanie. I'm gonna put it all behind me because I want a lovely life like yours."

It was as if a spark within Susan had suddenly been lit, like a burning hunger or driving ambition. She suddenly realised that she wasn't the only one to suffer, other women had been there too, and they had survived. As my experience showed her, it was possible to change the course of your life: the way forward was to refuse to let the past shape her future.

Her behaviour changed completely. From then on, she knuckled down to a routine with Jack every day. There were a few rare lapses, but nothing to merit a report to Carol and Janet.

Whenever Jack cried, that knot of anxiety over whether Susan would see to him or not had vanished. She would always be there, soothing or feeding him. I never heard another peep out of her about disgusting nappies.

The kids loved joining in with baby Jack, too, and their relationship with Susan became calmer, more mellow and fun.

One day I heard the sound of splashing and giggles in the bathroom.

I peeped in to see Susan, Sarah and Sophie preparing the baby bath, while Jack watched, fascinated, as the bubbles Stevie was blowing bobbed through the air.

It was so heartwarming to see Susan showing the girls how to test the water temperature with her elbow before she carefully lowered a gurgling Jack into the bath.

"He's a water baby, Mum," Sarah smiled as Jack's sploshing arms and legs tipped water over the sides of the bath.

"You were just the same when you were babies, girls," I said, recalling fun-filled bathtimes in the sink at Nana Ivy's.

There was a feeling of tranquillity in the house, now, and a sense that I could happily leave Susan to get on with it. When Jack started to crawl, she watched him like a hawk, making sure he never came to harm, that he was always safe.

As another Christmas drew near, mum and baby had become part of the fabric of our family, and we all shared in the festive excitement.

"Bed time," I said softly after we had all enjoyed the traditional annual merriment of decorating the tree.

This year, there was no argument about who should place the final ornament on top. "If you make a wish it will come true," said Sarah, holding out our battered angel to Susan. I had never felt so proud of my daughter. But then Susan made my heart swell even more. "Let's both do it," she smiled. "We can hold a wing each."

It wouldn't be the first time that Susan had made me cry, but this time, as I watched the two girls carefully place the angel on our tree, they were tears of joy. What a journey we had all been on. And now I had every reason to believe that Susan could make a good life with her son. I looked across at Bill, my rock, and we shared a conspiratorial smile.

It had been a long, emotional day and as I tidied up the bathroom, I was looking forward to putting my feet up.

"Need a hand?" asked Bill, poking his head around the door.

I shook my head.

"Let's have a night cap," I smiled. "Just you and me, on the sofa with a bit of White Christmas in the background."

Bill's eyes lit up.

"Fancy a glass of mulled wine, love?" he laughed. "Extra spicy?"

I squeezed his hand.

"It's going to be another lively Christmas in our house this year," I grinned. Soon, we would be filling five stockings ready for the next day. I couldn't wait for their whoops of excitement as they tore off the wrapping paper. I wondered if Susan had ever had a proper Christmas.

I will never forget the look on her face next morning when she realised that she had her very own stocking. But my own face must have also been a picture when Susan handed me a present. "That's for you," she said shyly.

I tore open the messily wrapped package to find a bottle of Aqua Manda foam bath. "Bill lent me the money," she said.

"Thanks love," was all my choked voice could muster.

Susan and little Jack stayed with us for almost a year before Janet assessed that they were ready to live independently. She got them settled in a little council flat in the next town.

"Can I keep in touch, Jeanie? I mean, if I need advice and that?" said Susan as we hugged goodbye.

"You know the answer to that, love," I smiled, welling up as Jack reached out from his mother's arms to give me a cuddle. "I'll always be there if you need me."

She handed me a paper bag. "So you don't forget us," said Susan. She gave me a quick, fierce hug and then she was gone, waving from the car until it disappeared around the corner. When I looked inside the bag I found a pair of Jack's tiny white booties.

Although my work with Susan and Jack was done, I missed them so much after they'd gone. The house seemed so empty without them. But she didn't disappear from our lives completely.

When she first left, we'd meet up once a month and when I saw what a good job she was doing as a single mum, I felt as proud as if she was my own daughter.

When Jack was old enough to go to nursery, she got a part-time job at a supermarket, as well as volunteering a few hours a week at a charity shop around the corner.

She didn't earn much, but with the little money she had, she would feed her boy healthy meals on a budget using the recipes she'd learned to make with Bill. The less spicy ones, of course…

As Jack was growing up, she made sure he never went without.

I marvelled at how, if she couldn't afford to buy him a new winter coat or the latest toys, she'd hunt high and low for the best bargains she could find at second-hand shops and jumble sales.

With a laser-like focus, she channelled her energy – which had previously fuelled her aggression – into raising Jack.

That little man was always immaculately turned out, a true credit to her.

"Do you think I'm a good mum?" Susan would ask me whenever a chink of doubt crept in.

"You're an amazing mum," I would reply. "I'm proud of you, love – and you should be of yourself."

Susan had changed her life around, truly transformed herself.

Sure, she was human like the rest of us, and would sometimes slip up. But not with drink or drugs or selling herself to a fella trying to bamboozle her with charm and a few quid. She was pretty wise that.

No, now it was usually her bad language that would let her down, spilling out unchecked in front of her boy if something had upset her.

"Careful, Susan," I'd gently chide and she'd put her hand over her mouth, mortified.

Jack was five years old when she found a new fella, a decent enough chap, and went on to get married. I was as pleased as punch when she invited me and our three children to the wedding. But what touched us the most was that she asked Bill to give her away.

With hope, pride and yes, a few tears, I watched Susan walk down the aisle in a white dress with little Jack as pageboy.

She went on to have two more kiddies, and although her marriage didn't work out in the long run, she was an excellent mum.

She was a little bit strict, too.

I would smile whenever I heard her berate her children with some of the same lines Bill and I used when she was a tearaway living with us.

"You're not going out dressed like that, young lady," she'd tell her teenage daughter. "Put some clothes on and cover up!"

She knew the pitfalls, the dangers, the risks out there, and all the tricks in the book that young people use to hoodwink their parents.

I can hardly believe that, like me, she's now a grandmother.

These kids are her life and, like any proud mum and grandma, she sends us their school photos and regular updates of what they're up to.

"Well done, Susan," I tell her. "You're an inspiration to them."

Looking back on our early days together, who would ever have thought that one day I would be telling her that?

Epilogue

The Troubled Trio

Not all of our children are success stories, like Susan; they don't all flourish, but when they do, it is incredible. It's so rewarding to watch children I helped through their most vulnerable times go on to have happy, fulfilled lives.

I form enduring bonds with some youngsters. My heart soars when they write or call to let me know how they're getting on. Listening to them talk about what they've done with their lives makes me so pleased and proud. We may have helped them along the way but in the end they did it themselves. And when you know how the odds have been stacked against them, it makes their achievements all the more remarkable.

One girl – who had rebelled against every rule and regulation going, and thought the police, or "bluebottles" as she called them, were the enemy – surprised us all by training as a police officer.

Another bright young lad made it to university and is now a qualified accountant; and then there's Keira, the troubled girl who now helps other youngsters like herself in her role as a social worker.

Being a foster parent is never easy, sometimes heart-breaking – but it's always worth it. Even at its most difficult…

Just as my family and I were adjusting to life without Susan and baby Jack, our link worker Carol phoned.

"Jeanie, I have an urgent placement," she said. "It's a real challenge, this one, but I think you'd be brilliant for it, the best woman for the job."

This became the preface to every case I took. But this one really needed me to be the right person at the right time: because, of all the cases in my 20 year career as a foster mother, this was easily the most harrowing.

"Okay, Carol, what are we dealing with?" I said, expecting to hear her describe a young girl in a similar predicament to Angela and Susan: a teenage mum in need of my maternal guidance.

However, nothing could have prepared me for what she told me next. Carol asked if I was prepared to foster three siblings – two sisters and a brother – who were being neglected and sexually abused by their own parents.

"They're very emotionally disturbed," she said. "The youngest sister hasn't spoken in over a year."

She explained that these poor kiddies – and the youngest in particular – had been through such extreme trauma that it had severely damaged their emotional and psychological health.

The children's so-called father, Dean Palmer, a big, brash bully of a man, already had form, serving time for ABH, GBH, rape and molesting underage girls.

Yet unbelievably, despite all the damning evidence against him, the youngsters' mother repeatedly refused point-blank to give him up.

"All three of them have behavioural issues," Carol told me. "We know, although we don't have any proof just yet because the children seem too scared to say too much about it, that the father has been sexually abusing the girls. Maybe their little brother, too."

Gary, who was six years old, still wet the bed and was terrified to sleep in his bedroom on his own. He'd been beaten up countless times by his dad and would pull his pillows out onto the landing next to his sisters' room to avoid sleeping in his own bedroom.

His sisters – Wendy, aged 12, and 10-year-old Tina – had not only been subjected to frequent bouts of casual violence from both their parents, they had also been exposed to explicit pornography watched by their dad at any time of night or day.

As a result, Wendy was very volatile, with serious anger issues, while her little sister Tina had become deeply withdrawn to the extent that she stopped speaking altogether.

I couldn't understand how any mother would sit by and let such prolific abuse happen to the three children she had carried for nine months, given birth to, and was supposed to love.

"What on earth is wrong with the woman?" I asked Carol. "How could she choose the father over them?"

"Amy Palmer is, it's fair to say, a bit of a tough nut, but she's been abused by Dean, too," she said. "She thinks his disgusting behaviour is normal."

Carol explained that Amy had been brutalised throughout her entire life, starting at puberty, when her father would beat and sexually assault her and her younger sister.

Although Amy hated her dad and couldn't wait to get away from home, she chose, in a calamitous twist, to elope with a man who was the carbon copy of her father.

"She's been totally brainwashed by Dean," said Carol. "It's hard for an outsider to understand unless they've seen it close up.

"Social services warned her that her kids would be taken into care if she didn't get him out of their lives – and she still chose him."

It beggared belief.

"Those poor kids," I said.

When I looked at Carol, I could see she was struggling to control her emotions, too.

"Even after all these years of working in social care, cases like this still affect me," she said, swallowing hard. "But that's how it should be, Jeanie. The moment you become desensitised and stop feeling, it's over."

I took a deep breath. If I accepted this case, my family and I would be dealing with not just one, but three damaged youngsters who had experienced some of the worst levels of abuse imaginable.

"Would this be a step too far for us?" I wondered. How we'd fit three extra kids in our little house was the least of our worries.

"There's something else you should know, Jeanie," said Carol. "The children will have supervised access with their parents, so if you take the kids on, you would need to meet them, too."

Later, I discussed it all with Bill.

He was filled with sadness, anger and disbelief when he heard what these youngsters suffered at the hands of the two people who should have nurtured, protected and above all, loved them most.

We knew we had to think long and hard before we took these kids on but, much as we could try and anticipate the challenges ahead, we would never really know what we faced until we were in the middle of it. For me it always came down to the same thing: a vulnerable child needed our help.

I looked at Bill. "So what do you think?"

He smiled. "We'd better get ourselves another set of bunk beds, hadn't we?"

In truth, I couldn't wait to welcome the siblings into our home: to get them away from the neglect and cruelty, and to prevent any further physical, sexual and mental abuse.

We knew we had a rocky ride ahead, but little did we know just how turbulent that journey would be.

My "troubled trio", as I now refer to them, would turn out to be the most disturbed youngsters I have ever met as a foster mum. It's comforting to this day to know that we brought them capsules of joy and peace of mind in the short time that they stayed with us. But the emotional rollercoaster we all experienced is a whole other story...

Acknowledgements

I'd like to thank Sally Morgan for bringing my story to life.

Also the Fostering Network for always flying the flag and encouraging government and people to give children in care a voice and a good standard of care.

Special thanks go to local authority fostering teams, who work so hard to protect children. And to ISP Fostering agency for helping foster carers to feel and be treated as professionals. The training and access to therapy for both carer and child has been invaluable.

For more information on fostering, visit:
thefosteringnetwork.org.uk